Meredith Books
1716 Locust Street
Des Moines, Iowa 50309–3023
meredithbooks.com

Printed in the United States of America.

First Edition.
Library of Congress Control Number: 2007942690
ISBN: 978-0-696-23397-5

Cover Photography: Robert Jacobs
Food Photography: Greg Scheidemann

the Deen Bros.

Y'ALL COME EAT

MEREDITH® BOOKS
DES MOINES, IOWA

Acknowledgments

A warm thanks goes out to those who shared their love and support and helped make our second book something we're truly proud of.

To our friends and family at The Lady & Sons Restaurant. Without Dustin Walls, Scott Hopke, Dora Charles, Rance Jackson, Cookie Espinoza, and the rest of the management and staff, we could not have done *Y'all Come Eat*. You make us proud every day.

To Melissa Clark, who helps two good-ol'-boy cooks shine like chefs.

To our team in New York. You're the best. To Barry Weiner and our literary agent, Janis Donnaud. Cheers, y'all.

To the creative team at Meredith Books for a wonderful, special experience: Erin Burns, Jan Miller, Mick Schnepf, and Lois White. Y'all did it again.

To Robert Jacobs and Greg Scheidemann for bringing this book to life with their beautiful photography.

And last but not least, a very special thanks and love to Mom and Dad.

From Jamie: All my love to Brooke and Jack, my two favorite people, and a big thanks to Coach Richt and the 2007 Georgia Bulldogs for making my son's first football game a great memory. Georgia 42 Florida 30. Gooooo, Dawgs!

CONTENTS

I've been lucky in so many ways,

and the biggest is with my family. I will not live long enough to express all the pride and love that I feel for my two boys. It's immeasurable. I'm so thankful and so proud that they continue to grow and become even better people with each passing day. They're not perfect, but they are good, kind men, and in my book that's the most important thing of all. People often ask me to give them advice on child rearing, and I can't do it! I just lucked up. Like most people their father and I made a lot of mistakes along the way, but Jamie and Bobby rose above it all. I guess the key has always been the undying love we feel for those boys. It shaped us as a family when they were small, and it shaped who they became as adults. And now it's a joy for me to watch them share their deep capacity for love with their own families and friends.

Of course as Southerners sharing the love also means sharing a meal. It's how we show our affection for each other. You may not have a lot of money to buy your family a bunch of expensive gifts, but you can always find the money to prepare their favorite dishes. With us Deens, food and family go hand in hand. We don't eat to live, we live to eat. And eating together is just about the best way for our family to spend time together.

And that's another way I got lucky. Because not only are my boys beautiful people inside and out, they also happen to be fabulous cooks. Even though Bobby, a bachelor, doesn't cook as much as the rest of us, when he does throw something on the grill it's always a feast and usually pretty healthy too. Being a family man, Jamie cooks on a more regular basis, and I often get to sample his cooking—it makes me bust out in a big grin every time! I think: That's my boy! He even knows how to make it look pretty. He's been working in the kitchen ever since we first started out with The Lady & Sons while Bobby worked on the floor greeting the customers. Both of them blossomed in their roles. Turns out Jamie had a real affinity for cooking and Bobby was the best host in Savannah. They made a great team back then and they still do.

That's part of why I love their latest book. It really captures that energy of how they are together. When you go to someone's house, it's not all about the food or all about the company; it's a combination of the two. And this book is a real portrait of that—great food and great folks coming together for a great time.

The other reason I love this book so much is because it's real. I flip through the pages and see all the people who are so important in Jamie's and Bobby's lives. There's Brooke and baby Jack, of course, and friends Dustin and Michael. It makes me feel like I'm right there with them, and that's the best feeling of all. It captures the memory of so many dinners, lunches, breakfasts, holiday meals—you name it, if we ate it, it's there as a memento for the future. I look at this book as more than a collection of my boys' recipes. It's a snapshot of their lives, one that they can pass on to Jack's generation. And when Jack looks at it, maybe he'll think of all the yummy things that make him say "mmmm" whenever he sees me coming and all the love we shared at every meal.

I hope it makes y'all inspired to cook something for your families too. As we Deens all know, there's nothing better than that!

Paula Deen

Growing up in the South—

especially with Paula Deen as your mom—means that making food is a
more than a hobby or just a way to feed the family. It's a way of life.

We were both cooking by age 7 and had already learned so much
just from being around Mama in the kitchen. Every day we would
come home from school, poke our heads into the pots, and ask, "When's
dinner?" And every night we would sit down to a fine, traditional, homey
meal such as Bobby's Goulash (Bobby's all-time favorite, page 169) or
Mama's Spaghetti Casserole (Jamie's weeknight standby, page 29).

These days the country seems to be heading away from a lifestyle that
allows people cook like that. Ours is a culture of convenience; we want
to be able to reach a hand out the car window and get a hot, fresh meal
that tastes great. But if we learned one thing from Mama, it's that there
is nothing as satisfying as the journey—the process of deciding what to
cook, picking out fresh ingredients, and making something from scratch.

Of course we are not exactly home with bread rising and beans
simmering all day every day either. When we're not on the road taping
our TV show, we are at the restaurant, and Jamie has a baby at home
so he doesn't get much downtime. That's why you can bet we know the
value of a quick-cooking meal that is still fresh and delicious. And we
sure appreciate that a can of tomato sauce, tuna, or even biscuit dough
can be a terrific base for homemade meals on a fast-paced timeline.

In Mama's kitchen early on, we learned that no matter what else is
going on, there is a way to make dinner most nights, and in exchange
for your effort you get not only a tasty plate of food but an opportunity to
connect with your life and, more importantly, the people in your life.

Cooking is definitely our main form of socializing. We enjoy being
in the kitchen so much, we wouldn't dream of keeping all the fun to
ourselves! Fixing food with friends and family is not only a faster way to
pull together a meal, it is also a way to take time for conversations with
loved ones, break the ice with friends of friends, and make everyone feel
included. You can bet baby Jack Deen will be right in there helping just
as soon as he learns to walk!

Some of the recipes we share in this book come from those casual
weeknights when Jamie and Brooke make recipes like Brooke's
Homemade Meatloaf (page 51) and English Pea Salad (page 53) for a
homey meal they can sit down to together after the baby is fed. Some of
our recipes are a little more dressed up. When Bobby has a date, dinner
at home is Plan A. His date-night recipes are more elegant, such as his
Bite-Size Tomato and Mozzarella Tarts (page 102) or the super easy but
extra delicious Grilled Tuna Steaks with Lemon-Pepper Butter (page 104).

The best part about our book is that it is so simple. If you are just starting
out, the recipes are easy to make. If you have been cooking forever, you

can still appreciate the simplicity of the flavors. But no matter what's on the menu, making food with that special someone is as much fun as eating it.

If we didn't love feeding people, it might be hard to keep the restaurant up to our standards, travel around eating and meeting for our TV show, and still find the energy to cook when we finally get home. But everything we do just makes us hungry for more good times, tasty meals, and great company.

At the end of the day, when you sit down with us for some all-out delicious homestyle eats, we're sure you will agree that nothing tastes better than your own cooking. Now, y'all come eat!

Bobby & Jamie

Quick and tasty weeknight meals for the family

GATHER THE

'ROUND TABLE

We will always recall coming home from school to find something wonderful simmering on the stove. We were on a budget, so weekday dinners were pretty simple—but ingredients were fresh and meals as good as they could be. Whatever Mama was cooking, we knew it would be comforting and delicious.

mondays

Startin' the Week Right

If you are used to eating plain baked chicken breasts, you will love our jazzed-up version with a creamy chile cheese sauce that is ready in about five minutes and packs a ton of flavor. Add some garlicky sauteed green beans and potatoes and you have something worth sitting down to. **Oh—and a little bacon never hurts!**

 MENU

BACON-WRAPPED CHICKEN BREASTS WITH
CHILE CHEESE SAUCE

RED POTATO AND GREEN BEAN SAUTE

Bacon-Wrapped Chicken Breasts with Chile Cheese Sauce

We love the intense, smoky flavor of chipotle peppers, which are actually dried and smoked jalapeños. Use more or less of the peppers depending on how sassy you like your food!

8   slices bacon
4   boneless, skinless chicken breast halves, cut in half lengthwise (making 8 long pieces)
1   10.75-ounce can condensed cheddar cheese soup
⅓   cup milk
1   teaspoon chopped canned chipotle peppers or bottled chipotle hot pepper sauce
         (or to taste)
         Dash Worcestershire sauce

1. Preheat oven to 400°F. Line a rimmed baking sheet with aluminum foil; set aside.

2. Wrap a slice of bacon around each piece of chicken and place on the baking sheet. Bake about 20 minutes or until cooked through. Remove chicken from the oven. Preheat the broiler.

3. Meanwhile, in a saucepan, bring the soup, milk, chipotle pepper, and Worcestershire to a simmer over medium heat. Turn off heat; cover to keep sauce warm.

4. Broil the chicken 4 to 5 inches from heat for 1 to 2 minutes or until the bacon is really sizzling. Serve chicken topped with the cheese sauce.

MAKES 4 SERVINGS

Red Potato and Green Bean Saute

This is that kind of down-home side that brings out the best of fresh produce, and this dish showcases two of our favorite vegetables: potatoes and beans, which are made even more special with a kick of garlic and a sprinkling of fresh basil.

	Salt
1	pound baby red potatoes, halved
1	pound fresh green beans, trimmed
1½	tablespoons extra virgin olive oil
1	clove garlic, minced
	Freshly ground black pepper
3	tablespoons chopped fresh basil

1. Bring a large pot of salted water to a boil. Add the potatoes; cook about 15 minutes or until almost tender. Add the beans; cook about 3 minutes more or until tender. Drain well.

2. In a large skillet, heat the oil over medium heat. Add the garlic; cook and stir for 30 seconds. Add the potatoes, beans, and salt and pepper to taste. Cook about 2 minutes more or until heated through, tossing to coat. Add the basil and toss once more before serving.

MAKES 4 TO 6 SERVINGS

Tuesdays

Tuesdays with a Twist

Bobby: We used to love freshwater fishing in landlocked southwest Georgia, but everything we caught was full of bones, so we hated the fish fry afterward! **Jamie's favorite fish is still a nice rare ribeye,** but after we moved to the coast I caught on to fresh seafood in a whole new way. I especially love tilapia because it is so mild and cooks in no time. Seasoned with garlic and lime and served with fluffy pilaf and asparagus, it's a light dinner full of protein and flavor—just how I like to eat most weeknights to balance out those occasions when I eat like it's my last meal on earth!

 MENU

BAKED TILAPIA WITH GARLIC AND LIME

ALMOND RICE PILAF

LEMONY ASPARAGUS

Tuesday

Lemony Asparagus

Asparagus is one of those veggies that can sing all on its own—or with some simple embellishments like you'll find here. When choosing stalks, pick those that are thin and bright green with tight tips.

2	tablespoons unsalted butter
1	pound thin, tender asparagus, trimmed and cut diagonally into 1½-inch pieces
	Juice of 1 lemon
½	teaspoon salt
¼	teaspoon freshly ground black pepper
	Finely grated zest of ½ lemon

1. In a large skillet, melt the butter over medium-high heat. Add the asparagus and toss to coat. Cover and cook for 2 to 3 minutes or until the asparagus is bright green and crisp-tender, shaking the pan occasionally. Stir in the lemon juice, salt, and pepper. Sprinkle with lemon zest.

MAKES 3 TO 4 SERVINGS

"Good to eat and good for you too, Lemony Asparagus goes with just about anything."

—Jamie

Wednesdays

Over the Hump

Jamie: When I was 16 I really wanted to go out with one of my best friend's sisters, so I invited her over for lunch. I couldn't believe it when she said yes! I made my finest spaghetti casserole, one of Mama's weeknight standbys. I started with a jar of sauce and added seasonings, nice big chunks of meat, pasta, and plenty of cheese and baked the whole thing until it was bubbling and delicious.

My date had seconds.

That relationship turned into a long-lasting friendship, and spaghetti casserole served with crusty garlic bread and salad with creamy ranch dressing is still my go-to meal whenever I need something simple that everyone will love.

MENU

MAMA'S SPAGHETTI CASSEROLE
WITH BAKED GARLIC HERB BREAD

ROMAINE, CUCUMBER, AND GRAPE TOMATO SALAD
WITH RANCH DRESSING

Thursdays

Gearing Up
for the Weekend

Bobby: You just can't argue with a good pork chop, but you can add sweet glazed carrots and a flavorful couscous salad for an extremely tasty dinner. We serve fresh pork chops that are unbelievably thick and flavorful at the restaurant. I like to make them at home the same way, going easy on the seasoning and searing them until they are really dark on the surfaces. Finishing them in the oven makes them especially moist on the inside. When I finish eating this meal, **there's nothing left but a bone for the dog!**

MENU

BOBBY'S SPECIAL SEARED AND BAKED THICK-CUT PORK CHOPS

BUTTERSCOTCH-BLACK PEPPER BABY CARROTS

COUSCOUS SALAD WITH FETA, TOMATO, AND OLIVES

Bobby's Special Seared and Baked Thick-Cut Pork Chops

Bobby's technique of searing the chops and finishing them in the oven gives them a tenderness we haven't found in any other preparation method. Purchase bone-in chops; the bones keep the meat extra moist and juicy.

4	12-ounce bone-in pork chops, about 1¼ inches thick
1	clove garlic, halved
	Salt
	Freshly ground black pepper
3	tablespoons extra virgin olive oil

1. Preheat oven to 350°F. Rub each chop all over with the cut sides of the garlic halves and season with salt and pepper. In a large ovenproof skillet, heat the oil over medium-high heat until shimmering. Sear the chops in the oil 3 minutes per side or until paper-sack brown.

2. Transfer the pan to the oven and cook for 4 minutes more. Let chops stand for 5 minutes before serving.

MAKES 4 SERVINGS

Butterscotch-Black Pepper Baby Carrots

2½	tablespoons unsalted butter		1	pound baby carrots, halved lengthwise
2½	tablespoons packed light brown sugar			Freshly ground black pepper
¼	teaspoon salt			

1. In a medium skillet, heat the butter, sugar, and salt over medium-high heat, stirring until smooth.

2. Add the carrots and toss to coat. Cover, reduce the heat to medium, and cook about 15 minutes or until the carrots are tender and glazed. Top with lots of black pepper. Serve hot or warm.

MAKES 4 TO 6 SERVINGS

Couscous Salad with Feta, Tomato, and Olives

DRESSING:

2	tablespoons extra virgin olive oil
2	tablespoons freshly squeezed lemon juice
¼	teaspoon salt
	Freshly ground black pepper

SALAD:

1½	cups water
1	teaspoon extra virgin olive oil
1	cup uncooked couscous
1	cup cherry tomatoes, quartered lengthwise
5	tablespoons sliced pitted kalamata olives
5	tablespoons chopped fresh parsley
4	ounces feta cheese, crumbled (about 1 cup)

1. For the dressing, in a small bowl, whisk together the 2 tablespoons oil, the lemon juice, salt, and pepper to taste; set aside.

2. In a medium saucepan, bring the water and the 1 teaspoon oil to a boil. Stir in the couscous; remove from heat, cover, and let stand for 3 minutes. Uncover and fluff with a fork. Pour dressing over the warm couscous and toss to combine. Add the remaining ingredients and toss gently to combine. Taste and adjust the seasoning if desired. Serve hot or at room temperature.

MAKES 4 SERVINGS

Recipes that taste like Sunday through and through

SUNDAY AND

DINNERS MORE

When we were growing up, Sunday supper took backseat to our restaurant duties. Now Sundays feel special to us—relaxing with the paper, then sitting down to a great meal with people we care about. When it comes to Sunday supper, there's nothing better than Mama's Fried Chicken Dinner with all the fixin's.

Sunday

Suppers

With Mama

We all remember when the tide turned on the chicken. It used to be that Dad and Jamie each ate a breast and Mama enjoyed the dark meat, and this went on for a couple of years. But when Bobby was about 10, he started saying, "I want a big piece of chicken." So Mama would eat the thighs, us boys would each have a breast, and Dad would have to pick at the wings and legs, then fill up on the sides. He was lucky that Mama's hoecakes and potatoes are so good!

MENU

MAMA'S FRIED CHICKEN

HOECAKES

QUICK PICKLED CUCUMBER, TOMATO,
AND ONION SALAD

HOMEMADE CREAMED POTATOES

Mama's Fried Chicken

Sometimes Mama adds a cup of hot sauce (Texas Pete® is her favorite) to the eggs before dipping the chicken. Just be sure to skip the cayenne if you want to try it.

1	4-pound chicken, cut into 8 pieces
1	teaspoon salt
½	teaspoon garlic powder
½	teaspoon cayenne pepper
½	teaspoon freshly ground black pepper
	Vegetable oil for frying
2	large eggs
¼	cup water
1½	cups self-rising flour

1. Rinse the chicken and pat dry with paper towels. In a small bowl, combine the salt, garlic powder, cayenne pepper, and black pepper. Using your fingers, rub the spice mixture all over the chicken pieces to coat evenly. Cover and refrigerate from 20 minutes to 24 hours (the longer the better).

2. In a large Dutch oven, heat 3 inches of oil to 350°F. Preheat oven to 350°F. In a shallow bowl, whisk together the eggs and water. Place the flour in a shallow dish.

3. Dip the chicken pieces first into the egg mixture and then into the flour, shaking off any excess. Fry the chicken, in batches if necessary, until golden brown and crisp on the outside and just cooked through (about 13 minutes for dark meat and about 10 minutes for white meat). Transfer chicken to a paper towel-lined plate to drain. Serve hot.

MAKES 4 TO 6 SERVINGS

✓

Hoecakes

The batter for these fluffy, skillet-cooked cornmeal cakes will keep in the refrigerator for up to two days. Make extra cakes to eat with syrup and butter at breakfast.

1	cup self-rising flour
1	cup cornmeal
2	large eggs
1	tablespoon sugar
	Pinch salt
¼	cup buttermilk
⅓	cup plus 1 tablespoon water
¼	cup (½ stick) unsalted butter, melted
	Vegetable oil or butter for frying

1. In a medium bowl, mix together all the ingredients except the oil.

2. In a large skillet, heat ⅛ inch of oil. When oil is hot, drop 2 tablespoonfuls of batter into skillet for each cake.

3. Cook cakes about 2 minutes or until crisp and brown on bottom; turn cakes over and cook about 1 minute more or until second side is brown. Transfer cakes to a paper towel-lined plate. Serve hot.

MAKES 15 CAKES

Quick Pickled Cucumber, Tomato, and Onion Salad >

2	cucumbers, peeled and thinly sliced		1	large tomato, cored and coarsely chopped
½	large Vidalia onion, thinly sliced		1½	tablespoons chopped fresh dill
1	tablespoon cider vinegar			Freshly ground black pepper
1	teaspoon salt			

1. In a medium bowl, combine the cucumbers and onion; sprinkle with the vinegar and ¾ teaspoon of the salt. Cover and let stand for 30 minutes.

2. In a separate bowl, toss the tomato with the remaining ¼ teaspoon salt. Add the tomato to the cucumber mixture. Add the dill and pepper to taste; toss to combine. Taste and adjust the seasoning if desired.

MAKES 4 SERVINGS

Homemade Creamed Potatoes

2 pounds russet potatoes, peeled and cut into 1½-inch chunks
  Salt
¾ cup milk
½ cup (1 stick) unsalted butter
  Freshly ground black pepper

1. Put the potatoes in a large pot with enough salted water to cover. Bring to a boil and cook about 15 minutes or until very tender. Meanwhile, in a small saucepan, warm the milk and butter.

2. Drain the potatoes and return them to the pot. Mash potatoes well with a potato masher; use a wooden spoon to beat in the buttery milk. Season to taste with salt and pepper.

MAKES 6 SERVINGS

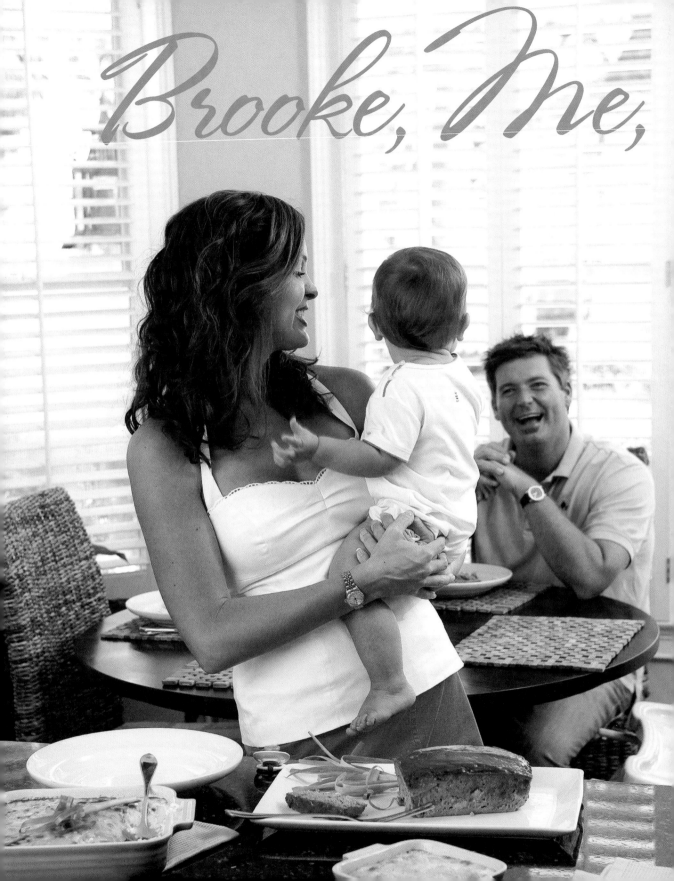

Brooke, Me,

& Baby Jack

Makes Three

Jamie: We want Jack to grow up seeing that his mama and daddy love to cook. And since he goes ballistic in restaurants at this age, we end up cooking at home together pretty much every day. From the way he has been getting into mashed banana, we think he may have the cooking gene!

MENU

BROOKE'S HOMEMADE MEATLOAF

THREE-CHEESE POTATO GRATIN

ENGLISH PEA SALAD

J

Brooke's Homemade Meatloaf

People always ask me, doing as much traveling as I do and with Paula Deen as my mom, what my favorite food is. I'm not saying that is an easy question to answer, but it always comes down to Brooke's meatloaf, which is moist and a little sweet. And she makes it with love.

MEATLOAF:

2	pounds ground beef (not too lean)
1	medium onion, finely chopped
3	tablespoons ketchup
2	large eggs
1	slice white bread, torn into pieces
1	teaspoon salt
¾	teaspoon freshly ground black pepper

GLAZE:

¼	cup ketchup
1	tablespoon Dijon mustard
2	teaspoons packed light brown sugar

1. Preheat oven to 350°F. In a large bowl, combine all the meatloaf ingredients; mix well. Press mixture into a 9×5-inch loaf pan. Bake for 30 minutes.

2. Meanwhile, in a small bowl, whisk together the glaze ingredients. After 30 minutes of baking, brush some of the glaze over the top of the meatloaf. Bake for 30 minutes more. Remove from oven and let stand for 5 minutes. Turn meatloaf out onto serving platter and spoon remaining glaze over top.

MAKES 6 SERVINGS

Three-Cheese Potato Gratin

Butter for coating dish
Salt
2 pounds red potatoes, sliced
   ⅛ inch thick
3 ounces Gruyère cheese, shredded
   (about ¾ cup)
3 ounces cheddar cheese, shredded
   (about ¾ cup)

3 tablespoons freshly grated Parmesan
   cheese
   Freshly ground black pepper
2 large eggs
2 cups half-and-half

1. Preheat oven to 400°F. Butter a 1½-quart gratin dish or shallow baking dish; set aside.

2. Bring a large pot of salted water to a boil. Add the potatoes; cook for 4 minutes (they will not be tender); drain. In a small bowl, stir together the cheeses.

3. Arrange one-third of the potatoes in the bottom of the prepared dish. Sprinkle with salt, pepper, and one-third of the cheese mixture. Repeat with a second layer of potatoes, salt, pepper, and half the remaining cheese mixture. Arrange the remaining potatoes on top.

4. In a separate bowl, whisk together the eggs. In a small saucepan (preferably one with a lip for pouring), heat half-and-half until steaming. Whisking constantly, slowly pour the half-and-half into the eggs. (If the eggs curdle slightly, just strain the mixture.) Season the egg mixture with salt and pepper; pour evenly over potatoes. Sprinkle potatoes with the remaining cheese mixture. Bake for 30 to 40 minutes or until the potatoes are tender and the top is golden. Let stand for 10 minutes before serving.

MAKES 6 SERVINGS

English Pea Salad

4 slices bacon
1 10-ounce package frozen peas,
   thawed and drained
4 ounces cheddar cheese, shredded
   (about 1 cup)

2 hard-cooked eggs, peeled and chopped
3 tablespoons mayonnaise
2 teaspoons freshly squeezed lemon juice
   Salt
   Freshly ground black pepper

1. In a large skillet, cook the bacon over medium heat until crisp. Transfer to a paper towel-lined plate to drain. Let cool.

2. In a medium bowl, combine the peas, cheese, and eggs. Crumble in the bacon. Stir in the mayonnaise, lemon juice, and salt and pepper to taste. Serve immediately or refrigerate until ready to serve.

MAKES 4 TO 6 SERVINGS

Early Bird

Special

Sunday Breakfast

The only thing better than waking up to a great breakfast on Sunday is making that breakfast for someone you care about—or everyone you care about. The smell of muffins baking and onions and sausage frying is the best alarm clock we can imagine.

MENU

PEACHES-AND-CREAM MUFFINS

JAMIE'S BREAKFAST CASSEROLE WITH HAM AND CHEESE

BERRY PARFAITS WITH COCONUT GRANOLA

'TATER SKILLET BREAKFAST

BOBBY'S EGG WHITE OMELETS
WITH SPINACH AND TOMATO

Peaches-and-Cream Muffins

We usually use sweet canned peaches in these tender, buttery breakfast treats, which are a cross between a biscuit and a muffin. But get your hands on some ripe Georgia peaches and you'll see why these are the most delicious muffins you've ever tasted.

	Nonstick cooking spray
2	cups self-rising flour
1	cup (2 sticks) unsalted butter, melted
1	cup sour cream
¼	cup sugar
1	teaspoon vanilla
1	15-ounce can sliced peaches, drained and chopped into ¼-inch pieces

1. Preheat oven to 350°F. Coat the cups of a 12-cup muffin tin with cooking spray; set aside.

2. In a large bowl, whisk together the flour, butter, sour cream, sugar, and vanilla. Gently fold in the peaches.

3. Divide the batter evenly among the prepared muffin cups. Bake for 30 to 35 minutes or until golden and a toothpick inserted in the center of a muffin comes out clean. Let muffins cool in pan for 10 minutes. Serve immediately or transfer to a wire rack to cool completely.

MAKES 12 MUFFINS

Jamie's Breakfast Casserole with Ham and Cheese

I can get very excited about a big breakfast casserole. Who wouldn't when the toast, eggs, ham, and cheese are all in one place? This recipe is my time-tested version with peppers and onions added for good measure. Because you can put it together the night before, you barely need to open your eyes before popping it in the oven.

	Butter for coating pan	1	6-ounce slab thick-cut ham, finely chopped
1	tablespoon extra virgin olive oil		
1	small onion, finely chopped	6	ounces Swiss cheese, shredded (about 1½ cups)
	Pinch salt		
1	medium yellow bell pepper, finely chopped (¾ cup)	5	extra-large eggs
		1¾	cups milk
1	medium red bell pepper, finely chopped (¾ cup)	¾	teaspoon salt
		¼	teaspoon freshly ground black pepper
1	8-ounce loaf hearty French or Italian bread, sliced ½ inch thick		

1. Butter an 8-inch oval or round baking dish.

2. In a large skillet, heat the oil over medium heat. Add the onion and the pinch salt; cook for 3 to 5 minutes or until the onion is translucent, stirring occasionally. Add the yellow and red peppers; cook for 3 to 5 minutes or until softened, stirring occasionally.

3. Cover the bottom of the prepared pan with half of the bread slices, cutting pieces as necessary to make a snug fit. Top the bread with half of the onion mixture, then half of the ham and half of the cheese. Repeat the layers, starting with the bread and ending with the cheese.

4. In a medium bowl, whisk together the eggs, milk, the ¾ teaspoon salt, and the black pepper; pour evenly over the casserole. (The egg mixture should come almost to the top of the pan.) Cover with plastic wrap and refrigerate overnight.

5. Let the casserole come to room temperature for 30 minutes. Preheat the oven to 350°F. Bake about 45 minutes or until top is golden and puffy and a knife inserted in the middle comes out clean.

MAKES 4 SERVINGS

< Berry Parfaits with Coconut Granola

½	cup sweetened flaked coconut	8	large fresh strawberries, hulled and sliced
1	cup granola	1	cup fresh blueberries
1	cup vanilla yogurt		
¼	cup honey		

1. Preheat oven to 325°F. Spread the coconut in a rimmed baking pan. Bake for 3 to 5 minutes or until golden brown, shaking the pan occasionally. Stir the coconut and granola together in a small bowl; set aside.

2. Place ¼ cup of the yogurt in each of two tall parfait glasses. Spoon 1 tablespoon of the honey in each glass, followed by 2 of the berries, then one-fourth of the coconut-granola mixture. Repeat, layering the rest of the yogurt, honey, berries, and granola mixture in the glasses. Serve with long spoons.

MAKES 2 SERVINGS

'Tater Skillet Breakfast

2	fresh hot or sweet Italian sausages (about 8 ounces), casings removed		Salt and freshly ground black pepper
1½	teaspoons vegetable oil	½	cup quick-cooking grits
4	cups frozen hash browns (from a 16-ounce package)	2	ounces cheddar cheese, shredded (about ½ cup)
		4	extra-large eggs

1. Crumble the sausage into a medium ovenproof skillet; cook over medium heat until brown. Transfer sausage to a paper towel-lined plate.

2. Add the oil to the skillet; cook the hash browns in oil according to package instructions, seasoning with salt and pepper.

3. Meanwhile, in a medium saucepan, bring 1½ cups salted water to a boil. Stir in the grits; reduce heat to medium-low. Cook about 5 minutes or until thickened, stirring frequently. Stir in the cheese.

4. Preheat the broiler. Using a slotted spoon, scatter the sausage over the hash browns. Pour the cheese grits over the sausage and smooth out the top. With the back of a spoon, make 4 shallow wells in the grits and break one egg into each well. Season the eggs with salt and pepper and put the pan under the broiler until the eggs are set to your liking (about 4 to 5 minutes for a medium-set yolk).

MAKES 4 SERVINGS

Bobby's Egg White Omelets with Spinach and Tomato

On weekdays I don't do much for breakfast—maybe a bowl of oatmeal or cold cereal. But on Sunday morning when I know I'm not going to do much of anything all day, that's another story, especially if I have company.

4	teaspoons extra virgin olive oil
1	small onion, finely chopped
	Salt
1	10-ounce package frozen chopped spinach, thawed, all excess water squeezed out
4	plum tomatoes, finely chopped (about 1½ cups)
	Freshly ground black pepper
12	egg whites
2	tablespoons water
	Nonstick cooking spray

1. In a small skillet, heat the oil over medium heat. Add the onion and a pinch salt; cook for 3 to 5 minutes or until onion is softened. Add the spinach; cook and stir until hot. Add the tomatoes, pepper to taste, and another pinch salt; cook and stir for 1 minute. Remove from heat; cover and keep warm.

2. In a medium bowl, whisk the egg whites, water, and a pinch salt until frothy. Lightly coat a medium nonstick skillet or omelet pan with cooking spray; heat skillet over medium heat. Add one-fourth of the egg whites, swirling to evenly cover the bottom of the pan. Cook for 1½ to 2 minutes or until set, using a rubber scraper to mix the eggs occasionally and to lift them up and let the runny egg flow underneath. Spoon one-fourth of the spinach mixture onto half of the omelet, fold over, and slide onto a plate. Repeat with remaining egg whites and spinach mixture.

MAKES 4 SERVINGS

Porch Sittin'

Snacks for Lazy Afternoons

Sitting on the porch, greeting friends and neighbors, and chatting away the time on a breezy Sunday afternoon is a fine Southern tradition and one we are proud to carry on—so long as the snacks keep up with the conversation!

MENU

CREAMY ARTICHOKE AND SPINACH DIP WITH PITA CHIPS

PIMIENTO CHEESE AND CELERY STICKS

EGG SALAD IN TOAST CUPS

JAMIE'S BEST HOMEMADE GUACAMOLE

DEEP-FRIED PICKLES WITH HONEY-MUSTARD DIPPING SAUCE

Season

Egg Salad in Toast Cups

8	slices soft white sandwich bread	¼	cup mayonnaise
2	tablespoons unsalted butter, melted	¼	cup chopped sweet pickle
4	hard-cooked eggs, peeled and coarsely chopped	2	teaspoons pickle juice
		½	teaspoon onion salt

1. Preheat oven to 400°F. Brush the edges of each slice of bread with the melted butter and place each in a cup of a muffin tin, pressing to mold the bread to the sides of the cup. Bake in the bottom third of oven for 7 to 10 minutes or until golden. Transfer toast cups to a wire rack to cool.

2. In a medium bowl, stir together the remaining ingredients. Divide the egg mixture evenly among the toast cups. Serve immediately.

MAKES 4 TO 8 SERVINGS

Jamie's Best Homemade Guacamole

2	ripe avocados, peeled, pitted, and coarsely chopped	⅓	cup sour cream
	Finely grated zest and juice of 1 lime	1	clove garlic, minced
1	medium tomato, finely chopped	½	teaspoon salt
1	small red onion, finely chopped	½	teaspoon freshly ground black pepper
			Tortilla chips

1. Place the avocados in a bowl and mash lightly with a fork. Add the remaining ingredients, except the tortilla chips; stir to combine. Mash avocado mixture to the desired consistency. Serve with tortilla chips.

MAKES ABOUT 2 CUPS

Deep-Fried Pickles with Honey-Mustard Dipping Sauce

The first time we had fried pickles, we knew they had to go on the menu at The Lady & Sons. If you've never had them—or heard of them—give them a chance. Crisp, salty, and fried, with a sweet-spicy dip they are everything you want in a snack.

HONEY-MUSTARD SAUCE:

½	cup sour cream
¼	cup Dijon mustard
¼	cup mayonnaise
2	tablespoons honey

PICKLES:

	Vegetable oil for frying
½	cup all-purpose flour
2	large eggs, beaten
½	cup cornmeal
	Salt and freshly ground black pepper
48	slices bread and butter pickles (from a 16-ounce jar)

1. For the sauce, in a small bowl, stir together all the sauce ingredients until smooth. (The dipping sauce can be made ahead and refrigerated until ready to use.)

2. For the pickles, in a heavy pot, heat 2 inches of oil to 350°F. Put the flour in one bowl, the beaten eggs in a second bowl, and the cornmeal in a third bowl; season the flour and cornmeal with salt and pepper.

3. Dip the pickles first in the flour, shaking off the excess; dip into the beaten egg, then dredge in the cornmeal to coat. Lay on a baking sheet. When all the pickles are coated, fry them in batches in the hot oil about 30 seconds or until brown. Using a slotted spoon, transfer fried pickles a paper towel-lined plate to drain. Serve pickles hot with honey-mustard sauce for dipping.

MAKES 6 TO 8 SERVINGS

Cooking for others is one of life's most rewarding activities

COME OVER

Maybe because we've logged so many hours in our restaurant, or maybe because we didn't eat out much as kids, when we have a choice, we always prefer to have folks over instead of going out. At the end of the day, there's no better feeling than knowing guests enjoyed eating a meal you made especially for them.

The Bru

nch Bunch

A Midmorning Meal
with the Usual Suspects

Sitting down for the first meal of the day when the sun is high and you have already read the whole paper is a real treat—especially when the company is great and the food is homemade and delicious!

RECIPES

CRAB EGGS BENEDICT

FRESH FRUIT SALAD WITH CREAMY CUSTARD SAUCE

TEXAS PETE® BLOODY MARYS

PEANUT BUTTER-AND-BANANA-STUFFED FRENCH TOAST

CHICKEN SALAD-STUFFED TOMATOES

CAT HEAD BISCUITS WITH SAWMILL GRAVY

√ *Crab Eggs Benedict*

Here we have the quintessential brunch dish, done up Georgia style with crabmeat and a hot sauce-spiked hollandaise. Poaching eggs can take some practice, so if you are new to it have a few extra on hand. Once you get the water to a nice gentle simmer, you will be able to slide in the eggs without losing too much white.

HOLLANDAISE SAUCE:

½ cup (1 stick) unsalted butter
3 large egg yolks
2 tablespoons freshly squeezed
   lemon juice
¼ teaspoon salt
   Freshly ground black pepper
   Several dashes bottled hot
   pepper sauce

CRAB AND EGGS:

¾ pound cooked lump crabmeat,
   thoroughly picked and cleaned
   of cartilage
2 tablespoons chopped fresh chives
2 tablespoons freshly squeezed
   lemon juice
½ teaspoon freshly ground black pepper
1 teaspoon white vinegar
6 large eggs
1 tomato, thinly sliced crosswise
6 English muffins, split, toasted, and
   still hot

1. For the hollandaise sauce, in a medium saucepan (preferably one with a lip for pouring), heat the butter until frothy. Use a spoon to skim off the foam. In a blender, whip the egg yolks, lemon juice, salt, pepper, and hot sauce for 3 to 5 seconds or until thickened. With the blender running, slowly pour in the hot butter, leaving the white milk solids at the bottom of the pan. Transfer the sauce to a bowl. Before serving, reheat the sauce in the bowl set over a pan of simmering water.

2. In a medium bowl, stir together the crabmeat, chives, lemon juice, and ½ teaspoon pepper; set aside.

3. Bring a large pot of water to a boil; add the vinegar. Crack each egg into a separate cup. Reduce the water to a simmer and carefully slide the eggs, one by one, into the water. Simmer eggs for 3 to 5 minutes or until firm. Using a slotted spoon, transfer the eggs to a plate lined with a clean dish towel.

4. Place a tomato slice on the bottom half of each muffin. Top each tomato with some of the crab mixture and a poached egg. Drizzle warm hollandaise sauce over eggs. Serve immediately with English muffin tops.

MAKES 6 SERVINGS

Fresh Fruit Salad with Creamy Custard Sauce

Fruit salad is fine for purists, but we like to jazz it up with a deluxe, almost dessertlike topping. To tell the truth, we would probably put custard on all our salads if we could!

1½	cups whole milk
6	large egg yolks
⅔	cup sugar
1	tablespoon vanilla
2	tablespoons unsalted butter, softened
6	cups mixed berries or other favorite fruit
	(such as chopped mango, papaya, pineapple, kiwi, pear, or banana)

1. For the custard, in a medium saucepan (preferably one with a lip for pouring), heat milk until steaming. In a medium bowl, whisk together the egg yolks and sugar until combined. Whisking constantly, slowly incorporate the hot milk into the egg mixture. Return the mixture to the saucepan.

2. Heat the custard over low heat about 5 minutes or until thickened slightly, stirring constantly. (It should be thick enough to coat the back of a spoon. Do not let the mixture come to a simmer or the eggs will curdle.)

3. Immediately strain the custard into a small bowl. Stir in the vanilla, then stir in the butter until melted. Serve fruit with the warm or chilled custard on the side, letting guests spoon the custard over the fruit as desired.

MAKES 4 TO 6 SERVINGS

Texas Pete® Bloody Marys

Bobby: I created my very own Bloody Mary recipe, keeping that first one I had in mind. I make them spicy, light, and zippy tasting. With a bunch of fat green olives at the bottom of the glass, this drink starts out tasting good and keeps getting better.

3	cups tomato juice
¾	cup vodka
2	tablespoons freshly squeezed lime juice
1½	teaspoons Texas Pete® hot sauce
1½	teaspoons Worcestershire sauce
½	teaspoon onion salt
½	teaspoon celery seeds
4	green onions and/or green olives

1. In a pitcher, mix together all the ingredients except the green onions. Pour into tall glasses over ice. Garnish with the green onions.

MAKES 4 SERVINGS

"The first Bloody Mary I ever had was also one of the best I ever had. On Hilton Head Island, Bloody Marys are packed with olives and savory seasonings."

—Bobby

Peanut Butter- and Banana- Stuffed French Toast

Jamie: I treated Brooke to a light breakfast in bed (see Berry Parfaits with Coconut Granola, page 61) one Mother's Day. Then later when we were hungry again, I came up with this over-the-top French toast full of everything you could crave for a sweet, hearty breakfast—all cooked into golden brown vanilla- and cinnamon-scented toast.

½	cup granola
8	slices white bread
¼	cup peanut butter
2	teaspoons honey
1	banana, peeled and thinly sliced
½	cup whole milk
2	large eggs
1¼	teaspoons sugar
½	teaspoon vanilla
¼	teaspoon ground cinnamon
1½	tablespoons unsalted butter
	Maple syrup

1. Preheat oven to 350°F. Place the granola in a shallow bowl; set aside.

2. Spread each slice of bread with peanut butter. Drizzle honey evenly over peanut butter. Divide the banana slices among four slices of the bread; top with the remaining bread, peanut butter sides down. Remove the crusts and tightly pinch the edges of each sandwich together to seal.

3. In a medium bowl, whisk together the milk, eggs, sugar, vanilla, and cinnamon. Soak each sandwich in the egg mixture for 5 seconds. Roll the edges of each sandwich in granola.

4. In a large skillet, heat the butter over medium-high heat. Add the sandwiches, working in batches if necessary; cook about 2 minutes per side or until golden. Transfer the sandwiches to a baking sheet; bake for 10 minutes. Serve immediately with maple syrup.

MAKES 4 SERVINGS

Chicken Salad-Stuffed Tomatoes

Stuffed tomatoes are usually one of the first things to go on a breakfast buffet, and they are elegant enough to serve at a sit-down meal. This recipe comes together in minutes, so the cook gets to sit down too.

2	cups shredded roast chicken
2	hard-cooked eggs, peeled and chopped
1	stalk celery, finely chopped
¼	cup mayonnaise
½	teaspoon salt
¼	teaspoon freshly ground black pepper
⅛	teaspoon garlic powder
4	large beefsteak tomatoes, cored

1. In a large bowl, combine all the ingredients except the tomatoes. Taste and adjust the seasoning if desired. Cover and chill chicken salad if not using immediately.

2. Just before serving, use a spoon to scoop out the insides of the tomatoes (reserve insides for another use). Divide the chicken salad among the tomatoes. Serve at room temperature.

MAKES 4 SERVINGS

Cat Head Biscuits with Sawmill Gravy

These biscuits are so named because they are the size of a cat's head! We have always enjoyed them with sausage gravy, which we call sawmill gravy in the South.

BISCUITS:

Nonstick cooking spray
3 cups self-rising flour, plus additional for dusting
1½ cups buttermilk
2 tablespoons unsalted butter, cut into pieces and softened

GRAVY:

1 pound bulk breakfast sausage
4½ tablespoons all-purpose flour
2¼ cups milk
½ teaspoon freshly ground black pepper
¼ teaspoon salt

1. Preheat oven to 400°F. Lightly coat a baking sheet with cooking spray; set aside.

2. For the biscuits, in a medium bowl, gently stir together the 3 cups flour, the buttermilk, and butter until the dough just comes together. On a floured surface, pat the dough into a 1½-inch-thick round. Cut the dough into six 4-inch circles; transfer to the baking sheet. Bake about 25 minutes or until golden brown.

3. For the gravy, in a large skillet, cook the sausage over medium heat until brown, breaking meat up with a fork as it cooks. Using a slotted spoon, transfer sausage to a paper towel-lined plate to drain. Pour off all but 2 tablespoons fat from the skillet.

4. Heat the remaining fat over medium heat and whisk in the 4½ tablespoons flour; cook and stir for 2 minutes. Slowly whisk in the milk; increase heat to medium-high and simmer about 3 minutes or until thickened. Stir in the sausage, pepper, and salt. To serve, split the biscuits and top with generous spoonfuls of gravy.

MAKES 6 SERVINGS

Saturday

Night

Doing Dinner Right

Bobby: Being a single guy I either have one friend over for a very nice dinner or do something casual with my buddies. But if I head over to Jamie and Brook's on a Saturday, you never know how much extended family will be gathering; it's not unusual to watch Jamie make a beautiful meal for 10 to 15 people.

RECIPES

CRAB-STUFFED MUSHROOMS

FIVE-VEGGIE, FOUR-CHEESE LASAGNA

HAM- AND CREAM CHEESE-STUFFED CHICKEN

CHOPPED CHEF'S SALAD WITH HOMEMADE
BROWN BREAD CROUTONS

SPINACH SALAD WITH WARM BACON DRESSING

GRILLADES AND GRITS

PESTO SHRIMP SALAD

Crab-Stuffed Mushrooms

Crabs are indigenous to the southeast coast of Georgia, so we love to put them in everything. These gems are perfect for a party and convenient too: Stuff the mushrooms and keep them in the fridge for up to six hours before you heat and serve.

4   ounces cream cheese, softened
3   tablespoons mayonnaise
1½   teaspoons milk
4   ounces cooked lump crabmeat, thoroughly picked and cleaned of cartilage
1   tablespoon finely chopped onion
1   tablespoon chopped pimiento
1   tablespoon chopped fresh basil
1   clove garlic, minced
¼   teaspoon freshly ground black pepper
⅛   teaspoon salt
24   white button mushrooms (about 1½ pounds), cleaned and stems removed

1. Preheat oven to 350°F. Line a rimmed baking sheet with aluminum foil; set aside.

2. In a food processor or with an electric mixer, whip or beat together the cream cheese, mayonnaise, and milk until smooth. Fold in the crabmeat, onion, pimiento, basil, garlic, pepper, and salt.

3. Spoon some of the crab mixture into the hollow of each mushroom; place on the prepared baking sheet. Bake for 15 to 20 minutes or until the filling is golden and puffed. Serve hot.

MAKES 24 MUSHROOMS

Five-Veggie, Four-Cheese Lasagna

This chock-full lasagna satisfies vegetarians and is hearty enough to satisfy meat-and-potatoes types. We like to keep this dish on hand in the freezer; well wrapped it will keep for up to four months.

	Salt
8	ounces uncooked lasagna noodles
3	tablespoons extra virgin olive oil, plus additional for drizzling
6	ounces portobello mushrooms, sliced into ¼-inch-thick pieces
1	medium zucchini, sliced lengthwise into ¼-inch-thick strips
1	red onion, sliced into ¼-inch-thick rings
	Freshly ground black pepper
1	14-ounce can artichoke hearts, drained and quartered

1	10-ounce package frozen chopped spinach, thawed, all excess water squeezed out
1	26-ounce jar spaghetti sauce
8	ounces ricotta cheese
4	ounces provolone cheese, shredded (about 1 cup)
4	ounces Parmesan cheese, freshly grated (about 1 cup)
8	ounces fresh mozzarella cheese, thinly sliced (about 2 cups)

1. Preheat oven to 375°F. Bring a large pot of salted water to a boil. Add the lasagna noodles and cook according to package directions until al dente; drain well. Arrange noodles in a single layer on a dish towel-lined baking sheet. Drizzle lightly with olive oil; set aside.

2. Spread the mushrooms on a baking sheet. On a separate baking sheet, spread the zucchini and onion in a layer. Drizzle 1½ tablespoons oil over each; season with salt and pepper. Roast until golden and caramelized (25 minutes for the mushrooms and 35 minutes for the zucchini and onion); cool. In a bowl, combine the vegetables with the artichoke hearts and spinach.

3. In a small saucepan, heat the sauce over medium heat for 5 minutes. Spread one-fourth of the sauce over the bottom of a 13×9-inch baking pan. Top with a single layer of lasagna noodles (about one-third), one-third of the ricotta, and an additional one-fourth of the sauce. Spread half the vegetable mixture on top of the sauce, then layer one-third of the provolone, Parmesan, and mozzarella on top of the vegetables. Layer on another one-third of the pasta, another one-fourth of the sauce, the remaining vegetable mixture, and another one-third of all the cheeses. Top with remaining pasta, sauce, and cheeses. Cover the lasagna loosely with foil. Bake 40 to 45 minutes or until bubbling and golden. Remove the foil, increase the oven temperature to 450°F, and continue baking about 10 minutes more or until the cheese is brown around the edges. Let stand for at least 10 minutes before serving.

Ham- and Cream Cheese-Stuffed Chicken

Bobby: This recipe comes from my good friend Amanda Stephens. She stuffs and coats the chicken breasts, then either fries or bakes them. You can probably guess which version I'm sharing with y'all. For a lighter variation, place the chicken on a baking sheet and roast at 400°F until the juices run clear when poked with a fork.

4	boneless, skinless chicken breast halves
1	8-ounce package cream cheese, softened
½	cup finely chopped ham
¼	teaspoon cayenne pepper (or paprika if you like it mild)
	Onion salt
	Freshly ground black pepper
	Vegetable oil for frying
½	cup all-purpose flour
2	large eggs, beaten
½	cup dried bread crumbs

1. Place chicken breast halves between two sheets of plastic wrap. Using a meat mallet or the bottom of a heavy skillet, pound halves until ¼ inch thick. Set aside.

2. In a medium bowl, stir together cream cheese, ham, cayenne pepper, and onion salt to taste. Mound one-fourth of the cream cheese mixture onto each flattened breast half. Pull the sides of the breast over the cream cheese and tuck in the ends. Use toothpicks as necessary to hold things together. (Don't worry if it doesn't look neat; this part will be on the bottom come serving time.) Season all over with additional onion salt and pepper.

3. In a large heavy pot, heat 2 inches of oil to 360°F. Put the flour in one bowl, the beaten eggs in a second bowl, and the bread crumbs in a third. Dip the stuffed chicken breasts first in the flour, shaking off the excess; dip into the beaten eggs, then dredge in the bread crumbs to coat. Carefully place the chicken breasts in the hot oil; fry about 8 minutes or until deep brown, turning once or twice. Using tongs, transfer chicken breasts to a paper towel-lined plate to drain. Remove toothpicks before serving.

MAKES 4 SERVINGS

Chopped Chef's Salad with Homemade Brown Bread Croutons

This is a salad like shrimp cocktail is a drink—in name only. More of a submarine sandwich in a bowl, this "salad" features crunchy croutons, cold cuts, olives, hard-cooked eggs, veggies, and cheese tied together by a zesty mustard vinaigrette.

CROUTONS:

1½	ounces brown bread, cut into ½-inch cubes (about 1¼ cups)
1½	tablespoons extra virgin olive oil
	Salt and freshly ground black pepper

DRESSING:

3	tablespoons red wine vinegar
1	tablespoon Dijon mustard
6	tablespoons extra virgin olive oil
1	clove garlic, minced
	Salt and freshly ground black pepper

SALAD:

3	heads romaine lettuce, chopped into bite-size pieces
4	ounces ham, cut into bite-size pieces
4	ounces turkey, cut into bite-size pieces
½	cup pitted kalamata olives, chopped
½	cup cherry tomatoes, halved lengthwise
2	hard-cooked eggs, peeled and chopped
1	cucumber, peeled and coarsely chopped

1. For the croutons, preheat oven to 350°F. Spread the bread cubes in a single layer on a baking sheet. Drizzle bread with the oil and sprinkle with salt and pepper. Bake for 12 to 15 minutes or until crisp and golden, tossing occasionally. Set aside.

2. For the dressing, in a small bowl, whisk together the vinegar and mustard. Slowly drizzle in the oil, whisking constantly. Whisk in the garlic and salt and pepper to taste.

3. For the salad, in a large bowl, toss together the salad ingredients and the croutons. Add just enough dressing to coat the lettuce and toss again.

MAKES 6 SERVINGS

Spinach Salad with Warm Bacon Dressing

This salad combines spinach, which is so good for you, with bacon, which is just so darn good! When you pour the warm dressing over the spinach, it shrivels just a little bit but is not cooked; it should still taste wonderful and fresh.

DRESSING:

5   slices bacon
1½   tablespoons finely chopped shallots
½   cup red wine vinegar
1   to 2 tablespoons honey mustard
     Salt and freshly ground black pepper

SALAD:

8   cups fresh spinach leaves, stems removed
8   ounces white button mushrooms, thinly sliced (about 2½ cups)
½   red onion, thinly sliced

1. For the dressing, in a skillet, cook the bacon over medium heat until crisp. Using a slotted spoon, transfer bacon to a paper towel-lined plate to drain. Pour off all but 2 tablespoons fat from the skillet. Heat the remaining fat over medium-high heat and add the shallots; cook for 2 minutes, stirring occasionally. Whisk in the vinegar, desired amount of mustard, and salt and pepper to taste, scraping the brown bits from the bottom of the skillet. Bring to a simmer; remove skillet from the heat.

2. For the salad, in a large bowl, toss together the spinach, mushrooms, and onion. Pour the dressing over the salad and toss to combine. Serve warm.

MAKES 4 SERVINGS

√

Grillades and Grits

Texans have their chili and Louisianans have grillades, a beefy Southern stew. This recipe, which is a favorite of Jamie, comes from a family friend named Hank Groover, who is a parish priest in New Orleans (we used to call him "Uncle Father").

GRILLADES:

3	pounds beef round roast, cut into 1½-inch cubes
1¼	teaspoons salt
1¼	teaspoons freshly ground black pepper
½	teaspoon garlic powder
6	tablespoons vegetable oil
3	tablespoons unsalted butter
4	stalks celery, finely chopped (2 cups)
1	medium yellow onion, finely chopped (½ cup)
1	medium bell pepper, seeded and finely chopped (¾ cup)
1	jalapeño chile pepper, seeded (if desired) and finely chopped (2 tablespoons)
1	clove garlic, minced
6	tablespoons all-purpose flour
3	cups beef broth
1	14½-ounce can diced tomatoes, drained
3	large tomatoes, cored and finely chopped (1½ cups)
2	tablespoons bottled hot pepper sauce
1	tablespoon Worcestershire sauce
1	teaspoon dried basil
1	teaspoon dried thyme
3	bay leaves

GRITS:

7	cups water
1	teaspoon salt
2	cups white grits, preferably stone ground
1	cup heavy cream
¼	cup (½ stick) unsalted butter
	Salt and freshly ground black pepper

1. For the grillades, season meat with ¾ teaspoon salt, ¾ teaspoon pepper, and ¼ teaspoon garlic powder. In a Dutch oven, heat 3 tablespoons oil and the butter over medium-high heat until sizzling. Brown the meat in batches. Transfer to a paper towel-lined platter to drain.

2. Pour off all but 3 tablespoons of the fat. Reduce heat to medium; add the celery, onion, bell pepper, jalapeño peppers, and garlic; cook for 3 to 5 minutes or until softened, stirring occasionally. Stir in remaining 3 tablespoons oil, then stir in the flour; cook 3 minutes or until pale golden. Slowly stir in the broth. Add beef, all the tomatoes, hot sauce, Worcestershire, basil, thyme, and bay leaves. Season with remaining ¾ teaspoon salt, ¾ teaspoon pepper, and ¼ teaspoon garlic powder. Bring to a boil; reduce heat to a simmer and cook gently for 1 to 1½ hours or until the meat is very tender. Discard bay leaves. Cover and keep warm over low heat while you prepare the grits.

3. For the grits, in a large saucepan, bring the water and salt to a boil. Stir in the grits; simmer about 15 minutes or until thick, stirring occasionally. Stir in the cream and butter; season to taste with additional salt and the black pepper. Serve the hot grits topped with the grillades.

MAKES 6 TO 8 SERVINGS

Pesto Shrimp Salad

Using purchased pesto is a great way to add flavor to dishes with no chopping and not much shopping. The green-flecked dressing complements shrimp beautifully; you could also substitute lump crabmeat or even chunks of leftover grilled tuna.

2	pounds medium uncooked shrimp, peeled and deveined
3	tablespoons crab boil seasoning
½	cup prepared basil pesto
1	stalk celery, finely chopped (½ cup)
¼	cup mayonnaise
¼	cup finely chopped bell pepper
3	tablespoons finely chopped red onion
	Salt and freshly ground black pepper
	Mixed salad greens

1. In a large pot, combine the shrimp and crab boil seasoning; toss to coat. Fill the pot with enough water to cover the shrimp by 2 inches. Heat over medium-high heat for 8 minutes (water does not have to come to a simmer or a boil). Turn off the heat, cover, and let the shrimp sit in the cooking liquid for 2 to 3 minutes more or until just opaque. Drain.

2. In a large bowl, toss the shrimp with the pesto, celery, mayonnaise, red pepper, and onion. Season with salt and black pepper to taste. Serve shrimp mixture at room temperature or chilled on a bed of mixed greens.

MAKES 4 TO 6 SERVINGS

"Everyone loves shrimp—especially me!"
—Bobby

Dinner

with Bobby

A Mellow Night In

Bobby: Anybody can make a reservation. When I want to show a friend a nice evening, I make dinner. Sometimes we'll do dinner on the end of my dock looking out on the ocean. I'll set up a table and we'll grill fish and just enjoy the quiet. That's my idea of eating out!

❧ MENU ❧

BITE-SIZE TOMATO AND MOZZARELLA TARTS

GRILLED TUNA STEAKS WITH LEMON-PEPPPER BUTTER

ZESTY CAESAR SALAD

Bite-Size Tomato and Mozzarella Tarts

Bobby: I have a big mixer on my kitchen counter. Truth is I don't bake all that often at home, but I don't mind letting people think I do! These simple little cheese and tomato appetizer tarts are a good example of the kind of baking that I will do!

	All-purpose flour for dusting
1	sheet frozen puff pastry (from a 17½-ounce package), thawed
1½	tablespoons freshly grated Parmesan cheese
1	large plum tomato, thinly sliced
	Salt and freshly ground black pepper
3	ounces fresh mozzarella, very thinly sliced (8 or 9 slices)
1	tablespoon chopped fresh basil

1. Preheat oven to 400°F. Line a baking sheet with parchment paper; set aside.

2. On a lightly floured surface, unfold the pastry. Using a 3-inch round cookie cutter, cut out 8 or 9 rounds; place rounds on the prepared baking sheet. Prick the pastry rounds all over with a fork. Bake rounds for 5 minutes. Remove from oven.

3. Sprinkle each with about ½ teaspoon Parmesan, then top with a tomato slice and season with salt and pepper to taste. Lay a slice of mozzarella on top of each tomato. Bake for 12 to 14 minutes or until puffed and golden. Sprinkle each tart with basil and serve warm.

MAKES 8 OR 9 TARTS

Grilled Tuna Steaks with Lemon-Pepper Butter

Bobby: I know of few fine meals that are as fast as grilled tuna steaks. Their only downfall is that they can get dry. Brief grilling and a pat of zesty butter will keep the fish moist and you happy.

2	tablespoons unsalted butter, softened
½	teaspoon finely grated lemon zest
1	teaspoon freshly squeezed lemon juice
¼	teaspoon freshly ground black pepper plus additional as desired
⅛	teaspoon garlic powder
	Extra virgin olive oil for brushing
2	6- to 8-ounce tuna steaks, about 1 inch thick
	Salt

1. In a small bowl, mash together the butter, lemon zest, lemon juice, the ¼ teaspoon pepper, and the garlic powder. Set aside (or chill if not using immediately).

2. Prepare the grill for medium-high direct heat and lightly oil the grate (or preheat a broiler). Brush oil on both sides of tuna steaks. Season the tuna on both sides with salt and additional pepper. Grill or broil for 3 to 4 minutes per side for medium rare, turning once.

3. Transfer tuna steaks to a serving platter; top with the butter mixture.

MAKES 2 SERVINGS

Zesty Caesar Salad

Bobby: My Caesar salad has a little bite to the dressing, and if you like you can add an anchovy or two. Even folks who claim not to like anchovies love the taste when they're blended in the dressing. Just don't tell them!

DRESSING:
1   ounce Parmesan cheese, freshly grated (about ¼ cup)
2   tablespoons freshly squeezed lemon juice
1   teaspoon Worcestershire sauce
1   clove garlic, coarsely chopped
¼   teaspoon bottled hot pepper sauce
¼   teaspoon salt
    Freshly ground black pepper
3   tablespoons extra virgin olive oil

CROUTONS:
1   ounce day-old country-style bread, cut into ½-inch cubes (about 1 cup)
1   tablespoon extra virgin olive oil
    Salt and freshly ground black pepper

SALAD:
1   head romaine lettuce, chopped into bite-size pieces
½   medium tomato, finely chopped (¼ cup)
1   ounce feta cheese, crumbled (about ¼ cup)

1. Preheat oven to 350°F. For the dressing, place the Parmesan, lemon juice, Worcestershire sauce, garlic, hot sauce, salt, and pepper to taste in a small bowl; whisk until smooth. Slowly add the oil, whisking constantly until combined. Taste and adjust the seasoning if desired.

2. For the croutons, toss the bread cubes with the oil and season with salt and pepper to taste. Spread cubes in a single layer on a baking sheet. Bake for 12 to 15 minutes or until croutons are crisp and golden.

3. For the salad, in a large bowl, toss the lettuce, croutons, and tomato. Add just enough dressing to coat the lettuce (save remaining dressing for another use) and toss again. Sprinkle with the feta.

MAKES 4 TO 6 SERVINGS

'meet at

the Grill

Guys' Night Out(side)

Even guys who don't like to cook inside will grill outside. We like to do both, but cooking out always guarantees a casual, fun time. Once you get your meat, there's not much else to do other than chill the beer and toss together a side dish or two. And there's not much cleanup either, which probably has something to do with why grilling is so popular with guys.

⤜ RECIPES ⤛

"BEER IN THE REAR" CHICKEN

STEAK KEBABS WITH PEPPERS, ONIONS, AND MUSHROOMS

GRILLED SAUSAGE- AND HERB-STUFFED PORK LOIN

GRILLED SPICE-RUBBED SHELL STEAKS

SMOKY GRILLED TROUT-IN-A-POUCH

GRILLED PARMESAN CORN ON THE COB

MIXED GRILLED VEGGIES IN A BASKET

"Beer in the Rear" Chicken

We learned the recipe from Mama, and it's a winner: The beer ensures that the meat comes out supermoist. We add a mayo rub to make skin nice and crisp. It just goes to show the magic you can work with a grill, a jar of mayo, and a can of beer!

¼ cup mayonnaise
   Finely grated zest of 1 lemon
1 teaspoon paprika
¾ teaspoon celery seeds
½ teaspoon salt
½ teaspoon freshly ground black pepper
   Pinch cayenne pepper
1 4-pound chicken, rinsed and patted dry
1 12-ounce can beer

1. In a large bowl, stir together the mayonnaise, lemon zest, paprika, celery seeds, salt, black pepper, and cayenne pepper. Slather the chicken inside and out with the mayonnaise mixture, place it in the bowl, and let stand in the refrigerator while you prepare the grill.

2. Prepare a charcoal or gas grill for indirect grilling. If using a gas grill, preheat the grill to medium and place a drip pan in the center of the grill. If using a charcoal grill, light the coals. When they are red-hot, use tongs to move them into two piles on opposite sides of the grill. Let coals burn until they are covered with a thin layer of gray ash. Set a metal drip pan in the center of the grill between the piles of coals.

3. When the grill is ready, open the beer can and drink a few sips (or discard). Put the can in the chicken's rear cavity, keeping the can upright. Stand the chicken upright on the grill grate over the drip pan. Cover the grill and cook for 1½ to 2 hours or until the chicken is very tender and nearly falling off the bone. (If using a charcoal grill, you'll need to add 10 to 12 fresh charcoal briquettes per side after 1 hour.) When done, the internal temperature of the chicken should register 180°F on a meat thermometer inserted in the thickest part of the thigh but not touching the bone.

4. Transfer the chicken to a cutting board or serving platter, taking care not to spill the hot beer. Let the chicken stand for 5 minutes; remove and discard the beer can and carve the chicken.

MAKES 4 TO 6 SERVINGS

Steak Kabobs with Peppers, Onions, and Mushrooms

You would be surprised how many ways you can use bottled Italian salad dressing—it is a great Southern shortcut. Here it creates an instant marinade that makes meat and veggie skewers moist, tender, and full of flavor.

8	skewers
2	pounds boneless sirloin steak, cut into 32 equal-size cubes
2	green bell peppers, cored, seeded, and each cut into 8 pieces
2	medium red onions, each cut into 8 pieces
16	white button mushrooms
1	cup bottled Italian salad dressing

1. If using wooden skewers, soak them in water for at least 30 minutes to prevent them from burning.

2. Build your kabobs this way: beef, pepper, onion, beef, mushroom, beef, pepper, onion, beef, mushroom. Place kabobs in a shallow dish. Pour Italian dressing over the kabobs and let marinate for 30 minutes at room temperature or up to overnight in the refrigerator, turning kabobs occasionally.

3. Prepare the grill for medium-high direct heat. Grill about 10 minutes or until the meat is brown and just cooked through, turning occasionally.

MAKES 8 KABOBS

Grilled Sausage- and Herb-Stuffed Pork Loin

We were in Houston, Texas, shooting an episode of *Road Tasted* when we first tasted a sausage-stuffed grilled turkey breast—it was something else. Being partial to pork, we took that recipe home and made it our own. Now we just can't stop making it.

¼	cup extra virgin olive oil	2	tablespoons chopped fresh basil
1	small yellow onion, finely chopped (⅓ cup)	1	4-pound center-cut boneless pork loin roast
3	hot or sweet fresh Italian sausages, casings removed		Salt and freshly ground black pepper
½	cup panko* or coarse bread crumbs	2	tablespoons chopped fresh rosemary
		2	cloves garlic, minced

1. In a large skillet, heat 1 tablespoon of the oil over medium-high heat. Add the onion; cook for 2 minutes, stirring constantly. Crumble the sausage into the skillet and cook until brown, breaking meat up with a fork as it cooks. Stir in the panko and basil; cook for 1 minute more. Let cool, then finely chop the sausage mixture.

2. Cut a vertical slit down the center of the pork roast, creating a 3-inch-deep pocket and leaving about ½ inch uncut at each end. Stuff the sausage mixture into the pocket. Wrap kitchen twine tightly around the roast to enclose the stuffing. Place the roast in a roasting pan and season generously with salt and pepper. In a small bowl, stir together the remaining 3 tablespoons oil, the rosemary, and garlic; coat the roast with herb mixture. Cover roast with plastic wrap and chill for at least 4 hours or overnight.

3. Let the roast come to room temperature while you prepare the grill for medium direct heat (alternatively, preheat oven to 500°F). Grill or roast the pork for 25 to 30 minutes or until an instant-read thermometer inserted in the thickest part of the roast registers 145°F, turning the roast every 10 minutes. Transfer roast to a cutting board and let stand for 5 minutes before carving.

MAKES 8 TO 10 SERVINGS

*Panko are crisp, coarse Japanese-style bread crumbs.

Grilled Spice-Rubbed Shell Steaks

Jamie: I grill a lot of steak. Steak sided with Tomato, Ham, and Cheddar Pie (page 176) is hands-down my favorite meal. Mama likes to butter her steaks, but I love to select a tender cut and give it a good spicy rub.

2	teaspoons dry mustard powder
1½	teaspoons dried oregano
1	teaspoon chili powder
¾	teaspoon salt
½	teaspoon freshly ground black pepper
2	20-ounce bone-in shell steaks, about 1½ inches thick
1	clove garlic, halved

1. In a small bowl, stir together the mustard powder, oregano, chili powder, salt, and pepper; set aside. Rub each of the steaks with the cut sides of the garlic halves, pressing the garlic hard into the bone to get the garlic juices flowing. Pat the spice mixture all over the steaks. Let steaks rest at room temperature while you prepare the grill or cover and refrigerate for up to 24 hours (bring the meat to room temperature before grilling).

2. Prepare the grill for medium direct heat. Grill the steaks for 6 to 7 minutes per side for medium rare. Transfer steaks to a cutting board and let stand for 5 minutes before serving.

MAKES 3 TO 4 SERVINGS

Smoky Grilled Trout-in-a-Pouch

Jamie: The first time I had trout I was about 14. We were in the Smoky Mountains and caught some fish, but all we had to season it with was butter and salt. That was enough. Even now anytime I have trout I remember Bobby, Daddy, Mama, and me eating on that mountain.

2   8-ounce boned whole trout
     Salt and freshly ground black pepper
2   tablespoons unsalted butter, cut into cubes
8   sprigs fresh thyme
6   thin lemon slices
     Wood chips, soaked for 30 minutes and drained

1. Rinse the fish and pat dry with paper towels. Season fish inside and out with salt and pepper. Scatter the butter cubes in the trout cavities and lay 4 of the thyme sprigs and 3 of the lemon slices in each. Wrap each fish in a double layer of heavy-duty foil.

2. Prepare the grill for medium direct heat. Scatter the wood chips in the grill. When they are smoky, lay the fish packets on the grill grate and cover grill. Cook about 3 minutes per side or until the trout flakes easily when tested with a fork.

MAKES 2 SERVINGS

Grilled Parmesan Corn on the Cob

This is a summertime staple for us. It is easy to prepare in advance and goes great with whatever else you are grilling.

¼ cup (½ stick) unsalted butter, softened
2   ounces Parmesan cheese, freshly grated (about ½ cup)
    Salt and freshly ground black pepper
8   ears corn, shucked

1. Prepare the grill for medium-high direct heat.

2. In a small bowl, stir together the butter, Parmesan, and salt and pepper to taste. Spread butter mixture evenly over the corn; wrap each ear in heavy-duty foil. Grill the corn, covered, for 10 minutes.

MAKES 8 SERVINGS

"We Deens love corn any which way, as long as there's lots of butter involved."

—Bobby

Mixed Grilled Veggies in a Basket

Grilling gives a meaty, savory flavor to food—even vegetables. We like the way the sweetness of the pineapple contrasts with the smoky grill flavor. This unusual combination might just get everyone hooked on grilled veggies.

½   cup tightly packed fresh basil leaves
½   cup extra virgin olive oil
2   tablespoons freshly squeezed lemon juice
1   clove garlic, coarsely chopped
    Salt
2   medium red or green bell peppers, seeded and quartered
2   medium onions (red, yellow, or Vidalia), cut into ½-inch-thick rounds
1   medium zucchini, cut into ½-inch-thick rounds
1   pint cherry tomatoes
1   pineapple, peeled, cored, and cut into ½-inch-thick rounds

1. Prepare the grill for medium-high direct heat.

2. In a blender or food processor, combine the basil, olive oil, lemon juice, garlic, and salt to taste; blend until smooth.

3. Brush or toss the vegetables (but not the pineapple) with half of the basil oil; arrange in a grilling basket. Place the pineapple in a separate grilling basket or directly on the grill. Grill about 10 minutes or until grill marks appear, turning once or twice. Serve the veggies and pineapple together on a platter drizzled with the remaining basil oil and additional salt if desired.

MAKES 8 SERVINGS

Great Big

Holiday Bash

We used to spend Thanksgivings at our aunt and uncle's home in the country. We would hunt and fish, then have a traditional Thanksgiving meal with oyster dressing, turkey, ham, green beans, and oh-so-many desserts. On Christmas Eve we would have dinner, then go to Granddaddy and Mama Deen's house for dessert and presents. On the way, we listened to the same radio program. The DJ would list Santa sightings, and we would look for him up in the sky. At night Dad would walk on the roof so we could hear his footsteps, and he would gobble up the milk and cookies we put out. Christmas morning we would be up by dawn, so when everyone else got up we were ready for a serious breakfast. Now that we are the cooks, we still try to make holidays special. Our recipes are a mix of classics and festive twists, and we always make more than enough—you never know who might need a midnight snack!

RECIPES

CLASSIC HOLIDAY BAKED HAM

CORN BREAD CASSEROLE WITH FRESH CORN AND GREEN ONIONS

MAMA'S FRIED PORK CHOPS

ULTRA CREAMY MAC AND CHEESE CASSEROLE

BLACK-EYED PEA SALAD

TENDER STEWED COLLARD GREENS

SAUTEED SQUASH AND ONIONS

PINEAPPLE AND PEACH CASSEROLE

Classic Holiday Baked Ham

Ham is definitely the holiday dish of choice down South. Slice up leftovers and serve on biscuits with scrambled eggs for one of the finest breakfasts either side of the Mason-Dixon.

1	10- to 14-pound bone-in, ready-to-cook ham
½	cup packed light brown sugar
2	tablespoons bourbon
1	20-ounce can sliced pineapple, drained
	Maraschino cherries (about 10) for garnish

1. Preheat oven to 325°F. Place the ham in a roasting pan and bake for 3 to 4 hours or until an instant-read thermometer inserted into the thickest part of the ham registers 150°F (about 18 minutes per pound).

2. Remove the ham from the oven and, using a sharp knife, make a crosshatch pattern, no more than ¼ inch deep, in the surface of the ham.

3. In a small bowl, stir together the sugar and bourbon until smooth; spread the mixture all over the ham. Decorate ham with pineapple rings and cherries, securing with toothpicks as necessary. Return the ham to the oven and bake for 30 to 45 minutes more or until the internal temperature registers 160°F.

MAKES 20 TO 30 SERVINGS

Corn Bread Casserole with Fresh Corn and Green Onions

Jamie: Fresh corn is one of my favorite things to eat. I eat it raw out of the field, I eat it roasted, I like it boiled, I like it baked, and this casserole has that delicious sweet fresh corn flavor that I love. The combination of fresh and creamed corn really puts the recipe over the top.

½   cup (1 stick) unsalted butter, melted, plus additional for coating pan
1   cup fresh corn kernels (from 2 ears of corn)
1   15-ounce can cream-style corn
1   cup sour cream
1   8-ounce package corn muffin mix
6   tablespoons thinly sliced green onions
¼   teaspoon freshly ground black pepper
    Pinch salt

1. Preheat oven to 350°F. Butter a 9-inch square baking pan; set aside.

2. In a large bowl, stir together the ½ cup melted butter, the fresh corn, cream-style corn, sour cream, muffin mix, green onions, pepper, and salt. Pour batter into the prepared pan. Bake for 60 to 75 minutes or until a toothpick inserted in the center comes out clean. Let stand for 5 minutes before serving.

MAKES 6 TO 8 SERVINGS

Mama's Fried Pork Chops

Mama can take something as simple as a pork chop and season, bread, and fry it so that it is knock-your-socks-off good. We like to make this for holiday meals, but what we like best is having it at Mama's—she breads the chops and slips them in and out of the pan with one hand while telling you a story with the other.

4	cups vegetable oil
8	8- to 10-ounce bone-in pork chops, about 1 inch thick
3	teaspoons salt
3	teaspoons freshly ground black pepper
1	teaspoon garlic powder
	Pinch cayenne pepper
	Pinch celery seeds
⅔	cup buttermilk
1⅓	cups all-purpose flour

1. In a large deep skillet or Dutch oven, heat the oil to 350°F. Arrange the pork chops in a large shallow dish. Season each pork chop with ¼ teaspoon salt, ¼ teaspoon black pepper, ⅛ teaspoon garlic powder, cayenne pepper, and celery seeds. Pour the buttermilk over the chops and turn to coat.

2. In a separate large shallow dish, stir together the flour, the remaining 1 teaspoon salt and the remaining 1 teaspoon black pepper.

3. When the oil is hot, dip each pork chop into the flour mixture and coat well, shaking off the excess. Using tongs, gently lower the chops into the oil, in batches if necessary. Fry for 8 to 10 minutes or until golden brown, turning once. Transfer chops to a paper towel-lined plate to drain. Serve hot.

MAKES 8 SERVINGS

Ultra Creamy Mac and Cheese Casserole

Here you have the Deen brothers' take on one of the most important—and delicious—casseroles we know. We have never had leftovers—it just doesn't happen.

¼	cup (½ stick) unsalted butter, cut into pieces and softened, plus additional for coating dish
2	cups uncooked elbow macaroni
8	ounces cheddar cheese, shredded (about 2 cups)
8	ounces American cheese, shredded (about 2 cups)
4	ounces cream cheese, cubed
1	cup half-and-half
4	large eggs
½	cup sour cream
½	teaspoon salt
¼	teaspoon cayenne pepper (optional)
	Freshly ground black pepper

1. Preheat oven to 350°F. Butter a 13×9-inch baking dish; set aside.

2. In a large pot of water, cook the macaroni according to package directions; drain. Return the macaroni to the pot. Add the cheeses to the hot macaroni and stir well; spread in the prepared dish.

3. In a medium bowl, whisk together the ¼ cup butter, the half-and-half, eggs, sour cream, salt, cayenne pepper (if using), and black pepper. Pour over the macaroni. Bake, uncovered, for 40 to 45 minutes or until golden brown and bubbling. Let stand for 10 minutes before serving.

MAKES 8 SERVINGS

Black-Eyed Pea Salad

Perfect for parties because it's great cold or at room temperature, this colorful salad is excellent with turkey or ham. And not that we're superstitious or anything, but black-eyed peas are supposed to bring good luck when eaten on New Year's Day.

2   15½-ounce cans black-eyed peas, rinsed and drained
1   large tomato, finely chopped (¾ cup)
6   tablespoons thinly sliced green onions
½   large red bell pepper, seeded and finely chopped (about ⅓ cup)
½   large green bell pepper, seeded and finely chopped (about ⅓ cup)
1   jalapeño chile pepper, seeded (if desired) and finely chopped (2 tablespoons)
¼   cup chopped fresh parsley
¼   cup chopped fresh basil
¼   cup chopped fresh cilantro
¾   cup extra virgin olive oil
¼   cup balsamic vinegar
     Salt and freshly ground black pepper

1. In a large bowl, stir together the peas, tomato, green onions, bell peppers, jalapeño pepper, parsley, basil, and cilantro. In a small bowl, whisk together the oil, vinegar, and salt and black pepper to taste. Pour the vinaigrette over the salad and toss to combine. Serve at room temperature or chilled.

MAKES 6 TO 8 SERVINGS

Tender Stewed Collard Greens

2   large bunches collard greens (about 4 pounds), stems and center ribs removed
2   quarts chicken or vegetable broth
1   cup (2 sticks) unsalted butter
2   tablespoons bottled hot pepper sauce
½   teaspoon salt

1. Stack the collard greens on top of each other, roll them up, and cut the roll into ½- to 1-inch-wide strips (do this in batches of 6 to 8 leaves).

2. In a large Dutch oven, stir together the broth, butter, hot sauce, and salt; bring to a simmer over medium heat. Add the greens; simmer, uncovered, about 1 hour or until very tender, stirring occasionally.

MAKES 8 TO 10 SERVINGS

Sauteed Squash and Onions

2   tablespoons vegetable oil
3   large onions, finely chopped (3 cups)
        Salt
2   pounds yellow summer squash, chopped
½   cup evaporated milk
1   teaspoon dried thyme
2   ounces Monterey Jack cheese, shredded (about ½ cup)
        Freshly ground black pepper

1. In a large skillet, heat the oil over medium-high heat. Add the onions and a large pinch salt; cook and stir for 3 to 5 minutes or until golden.

2. Add the squash; cook for 5 to 7 minutes or until softened but not mushy. Add the evaporated milk and thyme; simmer for 1 minute. Remove from heat and stir in the cheese, another pinch salt, and pepper to taste.

MAKES 8 SERVINGS

Pineapple and Peach Casserole

If you can take what is basically a cobbler and call it a side dish, we are all for it. For convenience take this sweet and savory family favorite to a function uncooked, then pop it in the oven when you get there.

½	cup (1 stick) unsalted butter, melted, plus additional for coating dish
½	cup packed light brown sugar
6	tablespoons all-purpose flour
8	ounces sharp cheddar cheese, shredded (about 2 cups)
1	20-ounce can pineapple chunks, drained (reserve 6 tablespoons juice)
1	20-ounce can peach halves in light syrup, drained and finely chopped
1	cup rich butter cracker crumbs

1. Preheat oven to 350°F. Butter a 2-quart casserole dish; set aside.

2. In a large bowl, stir together the sugar and flour. Gradually stir in the cheese. Add the pineapple chunks and peaches; stir until well combined. Pour the mixture into the prepared casserole.

3. In medium bowl, stir together the ½ cup melted butter, reserved pineapple juice, and the cracker crumbs, stirring with a rubber scraper until evenly blended. Spread crumb mixture on top of pineapple mixture. Bake for 35 to 45 minutes or until golden brown and bubbling. Let stand for 5 minutes before serving.

MAKES 8 SERVINGS

"Sweet from the fruit, salty from the cheese, this casserole really perks up a party."

—Bobby

IT UP GO!

No matter the season—hot, muggy summer or crisp, beautiful fall—picnics and potlucks are big in the South. And you don't show up empty-handed. So we keep a slew of recipes for crowd-pleasing dishes handy. Bottom line, if you tell a Deen to bring food, you better be hungry—we're going to be doing some serious cooking!

Marinating

Grilling and Swilling at the Game

It is so easy to be disappointed by professional athletes, but college football is pure athleticism—plus there's the tailgating, which is no casual affair in these parts. Guys go down the night before a game to pick out a good spot; they bring tents, TVs—with generators to run them—and grills, of course. We tend to focus on the latter, and we tailgate hard, making meaty favorites and bringing along plenty of beverages to toast the winning team or anything else that seems to need toasting. There just aren't enough Saturdays in the season.

MENU

NORTH CAROLINA-STYLE SPICY PULLED PORK SANDWICHES

FAVORITE SAUSAGE-POTATO SALAD

GARLIC-BUTTER BURGERS

DOWN-HOME COLESLAW

PICKLED SHRIMP IN A JAR

North Carolina-Style Spicy Pulled Pork Sandwiches

PORK:

1	tablespoon salt
1	teaspoon garlic powder
½	teaspoon freshly ground black pepper
	Pinch crushed red pepper flakes
	Pinch celery seeds
1	7-pound boneless pork shoulder, skin and fat left intact
	Down-Home Coleslaw (see recipe, page 143)
	10 to 12 soft buns

BASTING SAUCE:

3	cups cider vinegar
1	cup ketchup
2	tablespoons dry mustard powder
2	tablespoons packed dark brown sugar
2	tablespoons Worcestershire sauce
2	teaspoons crushed red pepper flakes
2	teaspoons salt
1	teaspoon chili powder
½	teaspoon freshly ground black pepper

1. For the pork, in a small bowl, stir together the salt, garlic powder, black pepper, red pepper flakes, and celery seeds. Using your fingers, rub the spice mixture all over the pork to coat evenly. Place pork in a large resealable plastic bag or a covered bowl; refrigerate overnight.

2. For the basting sauce, in a large saucepan, combine all the sauce ingredients, stirring to dissolve the sugar. Bring to a simmer over medium heat; simmer for 3 minutes. Let sauce cool; cover and refrigerate overnight.

3. Preheat oven to 300°F. Place a rack inside a large roasting pan; place the pork on the rack. Roast for 2½ hours; pour half of the sauce over the pork. Bake for 1 to 2 hours more or until an instant-read thermometer inserted in the thickest part of the roast registers 180°F, basting pork every 30 minutes with sauce and drippings from the bottom of the pan.

4. Remove pork from the oven and let stand on the rack until cool enough to handle. Meanwhile, warm the remaining sauce in a saucepan over low heat. Transfer the warm pork to a cutting board and shred or chop the meat into bite-size pieces, mixing in some of the fat and skin. Transfer pork to a large bowl; add sauce to taste and mix well.

5. Serve the pork on buns with Down-Home Coleslaw, passing any remaining sauce on the side.

MAKES 10 TO 12 SERVINGS

Favorite Sausage-Potato Salad

Bobby: One Christmas morning we went to Mama's for breakfast and gifts. She was frying up sausage, and I enjoyed it so much that I couldn't stop talking about it. When I went to get my stocking, I found a tube of sausage that Mama had secretly stuffed in there. The next day it went into potato salad, and I have been making it ever since.

SALAD:

1	pound red potatoes
2	teaspoons extra virgin olive oil
8	ounces kielbasa, sliced into ¼-inch-thick rounds
1	stalk celery, finely chopped (½ cup)
2	green onions, thinly sliced (¼ cup)

DRESSING:

1½	tablespoons red wine vinegar
1	tablespoon Dijon mustard
1	clove garlic, minced
¼	teaspoon salt
¼	teaspoon freshly ground black pepper
3	tablespoons extra virgin olive oil

1. Bring a large pot of water to a boil. Add the potatoes; boil about 25 minutes or until tender. Drain and let cool. Cut potatoes into quarters and place in a large bowl.

2. In a large skillet, heat the 2 teaspoons oil over medium-high heat. Brown the kielbasa. Transfer to a paper towel-lined plate to drain. Add kielbasa to the bowl with the potatoes.

3. For the dressing, in a small bowl, whisk together the vinegar, mustard, garlic, salt, and pepper. Slowly whisk in the 3 tablespoons oil. Add the dressing, celery, and green onions to the potato mixture and toss to combine. Serve warm or at room temperature.

MAKES 4 TO 6 SERVINGS

"Use your favorite sausage and lots of it here. For the record, mine is kielbasa."

—Jamie

Garlic-Butter Burgers

Our cousin Jay, who is a pretty health-conscious guy, was at Mama's house once and was watching her put chunks of something white into burger meat. He was very suspicious, but Mama told him that it was just garlic so he ate it up. He raved, having no idea until later that he was eating one of Mama's famous butter burgers!

¼	cup (½ stick) unsalted butter, softened
2	tablespoons chopped fresh parsley
1	large clove garlic, minced
	Finely grated zest of 1 lemon
2	pounds ground beef
1	teaspoon salt
1	teaspoon freshly ground black pepper
4	hamburger buns, split and toasted
	Tomato slices (optional)
	Onion slices (optional)
	Lettuce leaves (optional)

1. Prepare the grill for medium direct heat or preheat the broiler.

2. In a small bowl, mash together the butter, parsley, garlic, and lemon zest. Form the mixture into a log, wrap in plastic wrap, and chill in the freezer for 10 minutes.

3. In a large bowl, mix together the beef, salt, and pepper. Form into 4 patties about 1 inch thick; place on a rimmed baking sheet. Cut a slit ½ inch deep into the side of each burger. Cut the butter log into 8 slices; tuck 1 slice into the slit in each burger, pressing it deep into the burger. Pinch the slits closed so the meat totally covers the butter.

4. Grill or broil the burgers for 7 to 9 minutes for medium rare, turning once. Top the burgers with the remaining butter slices and place in the toasted buns. If desired, top with tomato, onion, and lettuce.

MAKES 4 SERVINGS

√

Down-Home Coleslaw

Tangy, sweet, and crunchy, this slaw is a must-have side or topper for a pulled pork sandwich (see recipe, page 138) and is indispensable for barbecues, picnics, and buffets. Be sure to let it stand before serving to blend the flavors.

1	1½-pound head cabbage, quartered, cored, and shredded
2	carrots, peeled and shredded (1 cup)
2	tablespoons chopped fresh parsley
2	tablespoons chopped fresh chives
½	cup mayonnaise
3	tablespoons finely chopped red onion
1½	tablespoons freshly squeezed lemon juice
2	teaspoons sugar
¾	teaspoon salt
½	teaspoon freshly ground black pepper
¼	teaspoon celery seeds

1. In a large bowl, toss together the cabbage, carrots, parsley, and chives.

2. In a small bowl, whisk together the remaining ingredients. Add to the cabbage mixture and toss well to combine. Taste and adjust the seasoning if desired. Let coleslaw stand at least 10 minutes before serving.

MAKES 8 TO 10 SERVINGS

Pickled Shrimp in a Jar

These tangy and sweet little shrimp need to pickle for a few days. Served with a cold beer, they make a great snack while you heat up the grill.

COOKING LIQUID:

8	cups water
1	large stalk celery, coarsely chopped (²⁄₃ cup)
1	large carrot, peeled and coarsely chopped (²⁄₃ cup)
1	medium onion, chopped (½ cup)
3	fresh parsley sprigs
3	fresh thyme sprigs
2	cloves garlic
5	peppercorns
1	bay leaf
1	teaspoon salt

SHRIMP:

2	pounds uncooked medium shrimp, peeled and deveined
½	cup cider vinegar
2	tablespoons freshly squeezed lemon juice
1	tablespoon sugar
2	teaspoons salt
1	teaspoon dill seeds
1	large onion, thinly sliced
12	whole peppercorns
6	bay leaves
6	cloves garlic
6	whole cloves

1. For the cooking liquid, in a large pot, combine all the cooking liquid ingredients; bring to a boil. Reduce the heat and simmer for 15 minutes. Strain, discarding the solids. Let the liquid cool in the pot.

2. For the shrimp, add the shrimp to the cooled cooking liquid. Heat over medium-high heat for 8 minutes (it is OK if it does not come to a simmer or a boil). Turn off the heat, cover, and let the shrimp sit in the cooking liquid for 2 to 3 minutes more or until opaque. Drain, reserving the liquid.

3. In a large bowl, whisk together the cider vinegar, lemon juice, sugar, salt, and dill seeds. Add the shrimp and let stand for 15 minutes.

4. In each of six 8-ounce jars, layer the shrimp and onion slices; add 2 peppercorns, 1 bay leaf, 1 garlic clove, and 1 whole clove to each jar. Divide the vinegar mixture among the jars. Top off each jar with the reserved cooking liquid. Screw the lids on tightly and store in the refrigerator for up to 3 days. Discard bay leaves.

MAKES SIX 8-OUNCE JARS

Gang's

All Here

Family Reunion Potluck

Our family loves an excuse to put together a real big meal, and we call on all the cooks to chip in. At weddings and funerals there is always more food than can be eaten. And for a reunion we put out all the greatest hits, from green beans and onions to eggplant Parmesan. These are dishes that travel well and reheat well. While you might not think it to look at them, somehow they all go together well too. Kind of like our family!

MENU

POT ROASTED BEEF WITH SWEET POTATOES AND CELERY

GROUND BEEF AND BAKED BEANS CASSEROLE

PICKLED BEETS SALAD

GREEN BEAN AND FRIED ONION CASSEROLE

KICKED-UP EGGPLANT PARMESAN

BANANA-DATE NUT BREAD

Pot Roasted Beef with Sweet Potatoes and Celery

Jamie: We grew up eating pot roast with potatoes. Now we try to limit white starches such as rice, potatoes, and bread (well, we attempt anyway). We love sweet potatoes so I thought I would try them with our pot roast—it turned out great. Baby Jack's first solid food was sweet potatoes, and he loves them. Wait until he tastes his first pot roast!

2	tablespoons vegetable oil
1	3-pound beef chuck roast
	Salt and freshly ground black pepper
1	10.75-ounce can condensed cream of mushroom soup
½	cup low-sodium chicken broth
½	cup dry white wine
½	cup water
1	medium onion, coarsely chopped (½ cup)
1	pound sweet potatoes, peeled and cut into 1-inch chunks
3	large stalks celery, cut into 1-inch pieces

1. Position oven rack in the bottom third of the oven. Preheat oven to 325°F.

2. In a large Dutch oven, heat the oil over medium-high heat. Season the roast with salt and pepper. Brown the roast on all sides in the oil.

3. Pour the soup, chicken broth, wine, and water over the roast; add the onion and stir. Cover the pot with a tight-fitting lid and transfer to the oven. Braise roast about 2½ hours or until tender, turning roast occasionally. Add the sweet potatoes and celery; cover and continue to cook about 45 minutes more or until the vegetables are tender.

MAKES 4 TO 6 SERVINGS

Ground Beef and Baked Beans Casserole >

Nonstick cooking spray
2 tablespoons vegetable oil or olive oil
2 large onions, finely chopped (2 cups)
1 pound ground beef
2 15-ounce cans Boston-style baked beans
2 medium tomatoes, finely chopped
   (1 cup)

¼ cup packed light brown sugar
1 tablespoon Dijon mustard
1¼ teaspoons salt
½ teaspoon freshly ground black pepper
5 slices bacon

1. Preheat oven to 350°F. Coat a 2-quart casserole dish with cooking spray; set aside.

2. In a large skillet, heat the oil over medium heat. Add the onion; cook about 5 minutes or until softened. Add the beef; cook about 10 minutes or until brown, breaking meat up with a fork as it cooks.

3. In a large bowl, combine the beef mixture with the remaining ingredients except the bacon; mix well. Pour beef mixture into the prepared casserole; arrange the bacon slices on top. Cover with a lid or aluminum foil. Bake about 45 minutes or until thick and bubbly. Uncover dish and preheat broiler. Broil for 1 to 2 minutes or until the bacon is crisp.

MAKES 8 TO 10 SERVINGS

Pickled Beets Salad

⅓ cup thinly sliced pickled beets
1 cucumber, peeled and thinly sliced
2 tablespoons mayonnaise
2 tablespoons sour cream
2 tablespoons chopped sweet pickles

1 tablespoon finely chopped sweet onion
1 tablespoon sweet pickle juice
¼ teaspoon salt
   Pinch freshly ground black pepper

1. Arrange the beets and cucumber decoratively on a platter (stripes, circles, whatever you like).

2. In a liquid measuring cup, whisk together the remaining ingredients; drizzle over the vegetables. Chill salad before serving.

MAKES 4 SERVINGS

Green Bean and Fried Onion Casserole

Sometimes veggies cooked in a covered dish can get too mushy, but these tender green beans and crunchy fried onions topped with cheese seem to complement each other perfectly.

¼   cup (½ stick) unsalted butter, plus additional for coating dish
3   cups chicken broth
2   cups cut fresh green beans
1   cup sliced fresh white button mushrooms
1   medium onion, finely chopped (½ cup)
2   tablespoons all-purpose flour
1⅓ cups heavy cream
1   2.8-ounce can french-fried onion rings
¾   teaspoon salt
½   teaspoon freshly ground black pepper
¼   teaspoon garlic powder
4   ounces Swiss cheese, shredded (about 1 cup)

1. Preheat oven to 350°F. Butter a 1½-quart casserole dish; set aside.

2. In a large pot, bring the chicken broth to a boil. Add the green beans; boil for 8 to 10 minutes or until tender. Drain, reserving the broth. Set aside beans and broth.

3. In a large skillet, melt the ¼ cup butter over medium-high heat. Add the mushrooms and onion; cook and stir for 5 to 7 minutes or until the onion is tender. Stir in the flour; cook and stir for 1 minute more. Slowly stir in the cream; cook and stir about 2 minutes or until thickened. Gradually add enough reserved broth until the sauce reaches a smooth, thick consistency.

4. Stir in the green beans, onion rings, salt, pepper, and garlic powder; pour into the prepared casserole. Bake for 20 minutes. Top with the cheese; bake for 10 to 15 minutes more or until the cheese is melted and bubbling. Let stand for 5 minutes before serving.

MAKES 6 TO 8 SERVINGS

√

Kicked-Up Eggplant Parmesan

When you are toting this sassy recipe to a function, take it warm and reheat it at 350°F for 15 minutes. Then sit back and watch everyone come for seconds.

1	26-ounce jar tomato sauce
2	tablespoons chopped fresh basil
¼	teaspoon crushed red pepper flakes
¾	cup all-purpose flour
3	eggs beaten with 1 teaspoon salt
2	cups dried bread crumbs
2½	pounds eggplant (about 2 large), trimmed and sliced lengthwise ½ inch thick
1	cup olive oil, plus additional as needed
1½	cups ricotta cheese
4	ounces Parmesan cheese, freshly grated (about 1 cup)
12	ounces fresh mozzarella, thinly sliced
	Salt and freshly ground black pepper

1. Preheat oven to 375°F. In a medium saucepan, simmer the tomato sauce, basil, and red pepper flakes over medium heat for 10 minutes; set aside.

2. Place the flour in one large shallow dish, the egg and salt mixture in a second, and the bread crumbs in a third. Dip each eggplant slice in the flour, shaking off the excess; dip into the beaten egg, then dredge in the bread crumbs to coat.

3. In a large skillet, heat the oil over medium-high heat until hot but not smoking. Fry the eggplant in batches in the hot oil about 3 minutes per side or until golden brown. Transfer the eggplant to a paper towel-lined plate to drain. Add more oil to the skillet as needed.

4. Pour one-third of the tomato sauce in the bottom of a 13×9-inch casserole dish. Layer one-third of the eggplant over the sauce. Top with one-third of the ricotta, one-third of the Parmesan, and one-third of the mozzarella. Season lightly with salt and pepper. Repeat layers until all of the ingredients have been used, finishing with a layer of mozzarella.

5. Cover the pan loosely with aluminum foil. Bake for 30 minutes. Remove the foil and bake about 15 minutes more or until the cheese is completely melted and light golden. Let stand for 10 minutes before serving.

MAKES 8 TO 10 SERVINGS

the Beach

Plus Fun and Frolic in the Water

Most of our picnics are beach spreads. We like to boat to the barrier islands with a big meal on board, eat the minute we get there, and jet ski as soon as everyone is ready. Then we polish off the leftovers and head home. Now that's the life.

MENU

CUCUMBER, VIDALIA ONION, AND CREAM CHEESE SANDWICHES

THREE + ONE BEAN SALAD

TOMATO SANDWICHES WITH DILLED MAYONNAISE

PEPPERONI CHEESE BREAD

MINTED LEMON AND LIMEADE

Cucumber, Vidalia Onion, and Cream Cheese Sandwiches

These might sound best for a dainty tea party, but they are full of flavor. We like to use a combo of white, wheat, and rye bread for a colorful platter of super satisfying sandwiches—they are perfect for just about any occassion.

2	ounces cream cheese, softened
¼	cup chopped, pitted kalamata olives
½	teaspoon freshly ground black pepper
8	slices white bread, crusts removed if desired
1	medium cucumber, thinly sliced
1	small Vidalia onion, thinly sliced

1. In a small bowl, beat together the cream cheese, olives, and pepper. Spread each slice of bread generously with the cream cheese mixture. Top 4 slices of bread with cucumber and onion. Cover with the remaining 4 slices bread. Cut sandwiches into halves or quarters.

MAKES 8 SERVINGS

"We live 60 miles from Vidalia, where these sweet onions were first grown. That makes it easy for us to recall just how good they make a sandwich taste."

— Jamie

Pepperoni Cheese Bread

If you're planning to take this savory, cheesy bread on a picnic, try to time it so it comes out of the oven about a half hour before you leave. Let cool for 20 minutes, wrap in foil, and serve warm when you get there. It's also terrific completely cooled, so you really can't lose with this recipe.

    Nonstick cooking spray
1   7.5-ounce package refrigerated biscuit dough (10 biscuits)
3   ounces cheddar cheese, shredded (about ¾ cup)
2   ounces pepperoni, chopped

1. Preheat oven to 450°F. Lightly coat a 9×5-inch loaf pan with cooking spray; set aside.

2. Flatten each biscuit slightly with your fingers; top with cheese and pepperoni. Pull the dough up and around the filling, pinching the edges to form a ball. Place the stuffed dough balls in the prepared pan (they should fit snugly).

3. Bake for 12 to 14 minutes or until golden brown. Serve bread while still warm. If packing for a picnic, cool 20 minutes on a wire rack and wrap in aluminum foil.

MAKES 1 LOAF

✓

Minted Lemon and Limeade

The real citrus and fresh mint in this recipe are a refreshing surprise coming out of a picnic thermos. It does taste best ice-cold.

4   lemons
3   limes
⅓   cup fresh mint leaves
¾   cup superfine sugar, plus additional as desired
8   cups cold water

1. Squeeze the juice from 3 of the lemons and 2 of the limes; strain the juice into a glass measuring cup (about 1 cup of juice). Thinly slice the remaining lemon and lime, removing the seeds; set aside.

2. In the bottom of a tall pitcher, use a wooden spoon to gently mash the mint leaves with ¼ cup of the sugar. Add the strained juice; stir well to dissolve the sugar.

3. Add the cold water and the remaining ½ cup sugar to the pitcher; stir well to dissolve the sugar. Taste for sweetness and add more sugar if desired. Add the lemon and lime slices. Chill before serving.

MAKES 8 TO 9 CUPS

THE ALL-TIME FAVORITE RECIPES

We are food people—always excited to taste something new. But we are fiercely loyal to a really good recipe. You know the one—jotted on an index card with little notes in the margin and a splotch of sauce over the most important part (but you know it by heart anyway). Every time we taste these dishes, we recall their origins, the people we have enjoyed them with, and all the good times and delicious meals gone by.

Bobby's Goulash

Bobby: Goulash was my favorite food growing up. Mama's goulash has macaroni cooked right into it, and you can bet she doesn't use lean beef. To this day Mama makes me a giant pot on my birthday. The rest of the year I make my own version; it's spicier than Mama's, with sour cream and jalapeños.

2	tablespoons extra virgin olive oil
3	pounds ground beef
2	large onions, finely chopped (about 2 cups)
2	14.5-ounce cans diced tomatoes
1	29-ounce can tomato sauce
3	tablespoons soy sauce
2	teaspoons dried basil
2	teaspoons dried oregano
3	cloves garlic, minced
1	teaspoon garlic powder
¾	teaspoon salt
¾	teaspoon freshly ground black pepper
2	cups uncooked elbow macaroni

1. In a large Dutch oven, heat the oil over medium-high heat. Brown the meat in the oil about 10 minutes, breaking meat up with a fork as it cooks. Add the onion; cook and stir for 5 minutes.

2. Add the remaining ingredients except the macaroni. Reduce heat; simmer, covered, for 20 minutes. Stir in the macaroni; simmer, covered, for 20 minutes. Let the goulash stand for 20 minutes before serving.

MAKES 8 TO 10 SERVINGS

Shrimp-Stuffed Twice-Baked Potatoes

Jamie: Mama has been stuffing baked potatoes my whole life, and I keep expanding on the theme. You can stuff a twice-baked potato with anything smaller than a potato, so use whatever sounds good to you: chicken and broccoli, leftover pot roast and gravy, steak or ground beef, or any kind of veggie. Use what you have on hand.

4	large russet potatoes (about 3½ pounds)
1	tablespoon butter
1	tablespoon extra virgin olive oil
2	cloves garlic, minced
8	ounces uncooked shrimp, peeled, deveined, and coarsely chopped
¾	cup sour cream
3	green onions, finely chopped (about ⅓ cup)
	Salt and freshly ground black pepper
4	ounces Parmesan cheese, freshly grated (about 1 cup)

1. Preheat oven to 425°F. Scrub the potatoes; prick each one several times with a fork. Bake for 45 to 60 minutes or until tender.

2. Meanwhile, in a skillet, heat the butter and oil over medium heat. Add the garlic; cook and stir for 30 seconds. Add the shrimp; cook and stir for 2 to 3 minutes or until opaque. Remove from heat; set aside.

3. When the potatoes are done and cool enough to handle, cut the top third off each one. Scoop the flesh out of potatoes and place in a bowl; add sour cream and mash. Stir in the shrimp, green onions, and salt and pepper to taste. Divide the potato mixture evenly among the 4 potato shells; top with Parmesan.

4. Place potatoes on a baking sheet. Bake about 15 minutes or until golden.

MAKES 4 SERVINGS

Mini Cheeseburger Puff Pies

The first time we ate filet mignon and blue cheese wrapped in puff pastry, we had an idea how to make it our own and a little more down-home. We use miniature burger patties instead of steak and cheddar instead of blue cheese. Finally we wrap the patties in purchased puff pastry for party-perfect finger food.

8	ounces ground beef
2	teaspoons ketchup
2	teaspoons Dijon mustard
¼	teaspoon salt
¼	teaspoon freshly ground black pepper
1	tablespoon extra virgin olive oil
	All-purpose flour for dusting
1	sheet puff pastry (from a 17.5-ounce package)
2	ounces cheddar cheese, shredded (about ½ cup)
1	large egg beaten with 1 teaspoon water

1. Preheat oven to 400°F. Line a rimmed baking sheet with parchment paper; set aside.

2. In a large bowl, mix together the beef, ketchup, mustard, salt, and pepper. Form the mixture into 8 equal-size patties. In a large skillet, heat the oil over medium-high heat until shimmering. Brown the patties in oil about 1 minute per side.

3. On a lightly floured surface, unfold the pastry. Cut the pastry lengthwise into four equal strips, then cut strips in half crosswise. Place one patty on each strip and top with cheese. Fold the pastry up around the burgers and pinch the edges together to seal, molding to fit around the patties. Brush the tops of the pastries with the egg mixture.

4. Place the mini burgers on the prepared baking sheet. Bake for 12 to 15 minutes or until puffed and golden. Let stand for 5 minutes before serving.

MAKES 4 SERVINGS

Easy Grilled Baby Back Ribs

Jamie: At the Salt Lick in Austin, Texas, I had the most incredible grilled ribs ever. I took the recipe and ran with it. I wound up with a dry-rub marinade that melts into a delicious, spicy glaze when you throw it on the grill. I thought, *"I'll never need another grilled rib recipe."*

2	tablespoons packed dark brown sugar
2	tablespoons paprika
1	tablespoon chili powder
1	tablespoon freshly ground black pepper
2	teaspoons garlic powder
¾	teaspoon salt
2	racks baby back pork ribs (about 2 pounds each)

1. In a small bowl, stir together all the ingredients except the ribs; set aside.

2. Using a sharp knife, cut and pull the membrane from the back of each rack of ribs. Using your fingers, rub the spice mixture over ribs to coat evenly. Place each rack of ribs in a large resealable plastic bag. Refrigerate overnight, turning bag occasionally. (If ribs will not fit in a bag, place on a baking sheet and wrap well with plastic wrap.)

3. Prepare grill for medium direct heat. Remove the ribs from the plastic bag and wrap each rack separately in a double layer of heavy-duty foil.

4. Grill, covered, for 25 minutes. Turn packets over; grill for 25 minutes more. Test for doneness by poking a fork between the bones; the meat should be very tender. If the ribs are not done, return to the grill and cook for 10 to 15 minutes more or until fork tender.

5. Carefully remove packets from grill. Unwrap ribs and place them directly on grill; cook for 2 to 3 minutes per side or until crisp. Transfer ribs to a cutting board. Let stand for 10 minutes before cutting into individual ribs.

MAKES 4 TO 6 SERVINGS

Tomato, Ham, and Cheddar Pie

This recipe began as Mama's classic tomato pie, which along with steak and grilled corn is Jamie's favorite meal. Sometimes we serve this for brunch because it goes great with eggs. Deens will probably make variations on this pie for generations to come.

1	cup mayonnaise
1	9-inch prepared piecrust (see recipe, page 209)
2	large tomatoes, finely chopped (about 1½ cups)
½	cup thinly sliced ham
3	green onions, sliced (about ⅓ cup)
¼	teaspoon salt
¼	teaspoon freshly ground black pepper
	Pinch paprika
8	ounces fresh mozzarella, thinly sliced (about 2 cups)
4	ounces cheddar cheese, shredded (about 1 cup)
1	tablespoon chopped fresh basil leaves

1. Preheat oven to 350°F. Spread the mayonnaise over the bottom of the piecrust. Scatter the tomatoes, ham, and green onions over the mayonnaise. Sprinkle with salt, pepper, and paprika. Top with the cheeses.

2. Bake about 30 minutes or until cheese is melted and bubbling. Let stand for 5 minutes before cutting. Garnish with chopped basil.

MAKES 6 TO 8 SERVINGS

Salmon with Butter-Lemon-Egg Sauce

We love to dress up fish with this zesty, tangy sauce, which is so good you almost want to eat it on its own. Try it on whatever is fresh at the fish store.

SALMON:

4	10-ounce center-cut skinless salmon fillets
	Salt and freshly ground black pepper
1	tablespoon vegetable oil

SAUCE:

¼	cup (½ stick) unsalted butter
2	hard-cooked eggs, peeled and finely chopped
2	tablespoons freshly squeezed lemon juice
1	tablespoon chopped capers
2	teaspoons chopped fresh tarragon or 1 tablespoon chopped fresh basil
	Salt and freshly ground black pepper

1. For the salmon, season both sides of the fillets with salt and pepper. In a large heavy skillet, heat the oil over medium-high heat until hot but not smoking. Cook the salmon in the oil about 4 minutes or until brown. Turn salmon over and cook about 3 minutes more or until just cooked through. (For well-done salmon, cook for an additional 1 to 2 minutes.)

2. While the salmon cooks, make the sauce. In a small saucepan, melt the butter over medium heat. Cook about 3 minutes or until the butter turns golden brown and smells nutty. Immediately remove pan from heat and stir in the remaining sauce ingredients. Serve sauce over the warm salmon.

MAKES 4 SERVINGS

Jamie's Vegetable Soup with Grilled Cheese Sandwich Dunkers

Jamie: Talk about a comfort food classic. Soup and grilled cheese just makes you feel taken care of and well fed. Sure, you could serve the soup on its own, but why not give the people what they really want?

SOUP:

3	tablespoons extra virgin olive oil
3	pounds ground beef
4	stalks celery, finely chopped (2 cups)
2	medium onions, finely chopped (1 cup)
1	28-ounce can chopped, peeled tomatoes, undrained
12	ounces fresh tomatoes, coarsely chopped (about 2 cups)
2	beef bouillon cubes
1½	teaspoons dried basil
1½	teaspoons dried oregano
1½	teaspoons garlic powder
1½	teaspoons salt
1	teaspoon celery salt
½	teaspoon freshly ground black pepper

2	bay leaves
4	cups frozen mixed vegetables
2	cups finely chopped white potato
1½	cups frozen corn kernels
1	cup frozen cut okra
½	cup uncooked elbow macaroni
¼	cup chopped fresh parsley

DUNKERS:

10	slices white bread, quartered and crusts removed
5	tablespoons unsalted butter, softened
10	slices American cheese, quartered

1. For the soup, in a large pot, heat the oil over medium-high heat. Brown the meat, in batches, in the oil, breaking meat up with a fork as it cooks. Using a slotted spoon, transfer the meat to a paper towel-lined plate to drain. Pour off all but 2 tablespoons fat from the pot. Heat the remaining fat over medium-high heat and add the celery and onions; cook until softened, stirring occasionally.

2. Add 3 quarts water, the canned and fresh tomatoes, the bouillon cubes, basil, oregano, garlic powder, salt, celery salt, pepper, and bay leaves to pot. Cover and simmer for 30 minutes.

3. Return the meat to the pot along with the remaining soup ingredients. Simmer, uncovered, for 45 minutes. Discard the bay leaves. Taste and adjust the seasoning if desired.

4. For the dunkers, spread each quarter of bread with butter. Place a slice of cheese between two pieces of bread (buttered sides out), pinching the edges together to seal. Heat a large skillet over medium heat. Cook the sandwiches about 3 minutes per side or until golden brown, pressing gently with the back of a spatula. Serve the dunkers with the soup.

MAKES 10 TO 12 SERVINGS

The Lady & Sons' Chicken Potpie

We put Mama's homemade potpie on the menu at The Lady & Sons from day one. It starts with a simple Southern stew, but when you make your own cream sauce and use fresh vegetables and a pastry top, you create a memorable, homey meal.

2	tablespoons extra virgin olive oil		2	chicken bouillon cubes
2½	pounds boneless, skinless chicken breast halves		2	cups frozen green peas
	Salt and freshly ground black pepper		2	cups cooked diced carrots
⅓	cup unsalted butter (⅔ stick)			Pinch ground nutmeg
½	small yellow onion, finely chopped (¼ cup)		¼	cup chopped fresh parsley
				All-purpose flour for dusting
2	cloves garlic, minced		1	sheet frozen puff pastry (from a 17.5-ounce package), thawed
⅓	cup all-purpose flour		1	large egg, lightly beaten
4	cups heavy cream			

1. Preheat oven to 350°F. In a large skillet, heat the oil over medium-high heat. Season the chicken with salt and pepper. Cook the chicken in the oil for 12 to 15 minutes or until cooked through, reducing the heat if necessary. Transfer the chicken to a paper towel-lined plate to drain. When it is cool enough to handle, chop it into bite-size pieces.

2. In the same skillet, melt the butter over medium heat. Add the onion; cook and stir for 3 minutes. Add the garlic; cook and stir for 30 seconds. Stir in the flour; cook and stir for 1 minute.

3. Slowly pour in the cream, then stir in the bouillon cubes. Stir in the chicken, peas, carrots, nutmeg, and salt and pepper to taste. Simmer for 1 to 2 minutes or until thickened. Stir in the parsley. Pour the mixture into a 9-inch round baking pan.

4. On a lightly floured surface, unfold the pastry and cut out a 10-inch circle. Using a sharp knife, lightly crosshatch the circle's surface. Place the pastry circle over the vegetables, tucking the excess dough down into the edges of the pan. Brush the crust lightly with the beaten egg.

5. Bake about 35 minutes or until the crust is puffed and golden. Let stand for 5 minutes before serving.

MAKES 6 TO 8 SERVINGS

Southern-Style Corned Beef and Cabbage

Mama's side of the family is Irish (Dad's side is Cherokee Indian), so we grew up eating corned beef and cabbage often. Mama always flavors this sweet-salty dish with some bacon (that's the Southern part). Every time we serve this dish, we look forward to a corned beef sandwich as a snack later that night.

1	4-pound corned beef brisket
3	cloves garlic
2	bay leaves
½	teaspoon bottled hot pepper sauce
4	slices bacon
1	head green cabbage, cut into 8 wedges
4	potatoes (1½ pounds), peeled and halved lengthwise
	Mustard

1. Rinse the corned beef under cold running water and place in a large pot or Dutch oven. Add the garlic, bay leaves, hot sauce, and enough water to cover. Bring to a boil. Reduce heat, cover, and simmer about 4 hours or until beef is tender.

2. Meanwhile, in a large skillet, cook the bacon over medium heat until crisp. Transfer the bacon to a paper towel-lined plate to drain, retaining the fat in the skillet. Add the cabbage wedges and potatoes in batches; cook over medium-high heat until brown but not tender.

3. When the beef is very tender, transfer it to a warm serving platter and cover with aluminum foil, retaining the cooking liquid. Add the potatoes to the simmering liquid; cover and simmer about 15 minutes or until they begin to soften. Add the cabbage; simmer about 15 minutes more or until potatoes are easily pierced with a fork. Discard bay leaves. Using tongs or a slotted spoon, transfer the vegetables to the serving platter and crumble the bacon over all. Serve with mustard.

MAKES 8 SERVINGS

These are our very best
sweets for your sweet

ENDINGS

What Southern boy can pass a table covered with cakes and pies without stopping to hang out and possibly embarrassing himself? We love to make special desserts for any occasion: company coming over, a birthday, a good movie on TV, a hot day begging for a bowl of ice cream, a cold day just made for baking … you get the idea! But what's even more satisfying is to see how happy homemade desserts make others. We like to make people feel special, and something sweet, like the recipes on these pages, does just that.

Tender Southern Pound Cake

Jamie: Mama made a lot of pound cakes while we were growing up. It was uncommon for there *not* to be one under a glass cake dome in the kitchen. And it is even more uncommon for me to walk by a pound cake without helping myself. I just can't seem to keep walking.

1   cup (2 sticks) unsalted butter, softened, plus additional for coating pan
2¼ cups sugar
     Pinch salt
6   large eggs
2½ teaspoons vanilla
     Finely grated zest of 1 lemon
1   tablespoon freshly squeezed lemon juice
3   cups self-rising flour
½   teaspoon baking soda
¾   cup buttermilk

1. Preheat oven to 350°F. Butter a 10-inch tube pan; set aside. In a large mixing bowl, cream the 1 cup butter with an electric mixer on medium speed. Add the sugar and salt; beat until light and fluffy. Beat in the eggs, one at a time, until incorporated; continue beating about 1 minute more or until frothy. Beat in the vanilla, lemon zest, and lemon juice.

2. In a medium bowl, whisk together the flour and baking soda. Alternately beat the flour mixture and the buttermilk into the butter mixture until well combined. Pour the batter into the prepared pan. Bake for 60 to 75 minutes or until a toothpick inserted in the center of the cake comes out clean.

3. Let the cake cool in the pan for 10 minutes. Carefully turn cake out onto a wire rack to cool completely before serving.

MAKES 10 TO 12 SERVINGS

Fresh Georgia Peach and Brown Sugar Ice Cream

Bobby: When we made ice cream as kids, Mama used to cut up ripe, sweet Georgia peaches fresh from the farm stand and throw them right into the ice cream machine. I remember the rhythm of our old ice cream maker churning—just the sound would get my appetite going.

3	large egg yolks
¾	cup packed light brown sugar
	Pinch salt
1½	cups heavy cream
1½	cups whole milk
1	tablespoon freshly squeezed lemon juice
2	teaspoons vanilla
1½	pounds ripe peaches (about 4 large), peeled, halved, pitted, and cut into bite-size chunks

1. In a large bowl, whisk together the egg yolks, sugar, and salt. In a large saucepan, bring the cream and milk to a simmer. Whisking constantly, slowly pour the hot milk mixture into the egg mixture until combined; return the combined mixture to the saucepan. Cook over low heat for 3 to 5 minutes or until the custard has thickened enough to coat the back of the spoon, stirring constantly. Immediately strain the custard into a bowl. Set the bowl in a larger bowl filled with ice water to cool, stirring occasionally.

2. Stir the lemon juice and vanilla into the cooled custard. Freeze in an ice cream maker according to the manufacturer's instructions, adding the peach chunks halfway through the churning process.

MAKES ABOUT 6 CUPS

Homemade Cherry-Chocolate Chip Ice Cream

Bobby: When I cook for a date, I like to serve ice cream. Ben & Jerry's Cherry Garcia® is my go-to flavor when I don't have much time, but for a special night I make my own. There is nothing more luscious than a bowl of freshly made cherry ice cream.

1	12-ounce package frozen dark cherries (2½ cups), thawed
½	cup sugar
6	large egg yolks
	Pinch salt
2	cups heavy cream
¾	cup whole milk
4	ounces miniature semisweet chocolate chips or chopped chocolate bar (about ⅔ cup)
1	tablespoon vanilla
1	tablespoon freshly squeezed lemon juice

1. In a small saucepan, stir together the cherries and 3 tablespoons of the sugar. Simmer over medium heat about 10 minutes or until the sugar dissolves and the sauce thickens slightly. Let cool. Transfer to a food processor and pulse until chopped but still chunky; set aside.

2. In a large bowl, whisk together the remaining 5 tablespoons sugar, the egg yolks, and the salt. In a large saucepan, bring the cream and milk to a simmer. Whisking constantly, slowly pour the hot milk mixture into the egg mixture until combined; return the combined mixture to the saucepan. Cook over low heat for 3 to 5 minutes or until the custard has thickened enough to coat the back of the spoon, stirring constantly. Immediately strain the custard into a bowl. Set the bowl in a larger bowl filled with ice water to cool, stirring occasionally.

3. Stir the cherries, chocolate chips, vanilla, and lemon juice into the cooled custard. Freeze in an ice cream maker according to the manufacturer's instructions.

MAKES ABOUT 1 QUART

Strawberry Shortcakes

Typically when Mama made strawberry shortcake, she used slices of pound cake topped with whipped cream and fresh berries. This recipe calls for split flaky cream biscuits instead. The cream biscuits are special on their own, so if you have any left over from the shortcakes, try toasting them the next morning for breakfast.

BISCUITS:

1⅔	cups all-purpose flour, plus additional for dusting
3½	tablespoons granulated sugar
1½	tablespoons baking powder
⅛	teaspoon salt
6	tablespoons cold, unsalted butter, cut into ½-inch cubes
⅔	cup heavy cream, plus additional for brushing
	Raw sugar for sprinkling
2	pints strawberries, hulled and sliced
3	tablespoons raw sugar
	Sweetened whipped cream

1. For the biscuits, in a food processor or large bowl, pulse or whisk together flour, granulated sugar, baking powder, and salt. Pulse or cut in the butter until the mixture resembles coarse crumbs. Pulse or stir in the ⅔ cup heavy cream until the mixture just comes together. Turn the dough onto a lightly floured surface and pat into a 1-inch-thick round. Wrap in plastic wrap and refrigerate for 1 hour.

2. Preheat oven to 350°F. Line a baking sheet with parchment paper. Using a 3-inch round cookie cutter, cut out 8 rounds from chilled dough. Place rounds on the prepared baking sheet. Brush with cream and sprinkle with the raw sugar. Bake for 20 to 25 minutes or until golden brown. Transfer the biscuits to a wire rack to cool.

3. While the biscuits bake, in a large bowl, toss the strawberries with the 3 tablespoons raw sugar. Let strawberries stand at least 20 minutes. To serve, split the biscuits and top with strawberries and whipped cream.

MAKES 8 SERVINGS

Peach and Cinnamon Cobbler

Spectacularly Southern, this cobbler is easier than pie! You may want to have some vanilla ice cream on hand, particularly if you are serving this warm.

Butter for coating dish

FILLING:

6	cups peaches, halved, pitted, and sliced ¼ inch thick
¾	cup sugar
¼	cup quick-cooking tapioca
1	teaspoon ground cinnamon
1	teaspoon freshly squeezed lemon juice
	Pinch salt

TOPPING:

1⅔	cups all-purpose flour, plus additional for dusting
3½	tablespoons sugar
1½	tablespoons baking powder
⅛	teaspoon salt
6	tablespoons cold unsalted butter, cut into cubes
⅔	cup heavy cream, plus additional for brushing

1. Preheat oven to 350°F. Butter a 2½-quart baking dish. In a medium bowl, stir together the filling ingredients. Pour filling into the prepared dish; set aside.

2. For the topping, in a food processor or large bowl, pulse or whisk together the 1⅔ cups flour, the sugar, baking powder, and salt. Pulse or cut in the butter until the mixture resembles coarse crumbs. Slowly add the ⅔ cup cream, mixing until the dough just comes together. Turn the dough onto a lightly floured surface and pat together. Form the dough into 2-inch balls. Flatten balls gently with the palm of your hand.

3. Evenly arrange the dough rounds on top of the filling. Brush a little cream over the rounds. Bake about 1 hour or until the biscuits are golden and the filling is bubbling.

MAKES 6 TO 8 SERVINGS

Apple Pie with a Sugared Lattice Crust

Bobby: I love to make desserts that look like a lot of trouble even when they're super simple like this apple pie. You can make a lattice from a frozen piecrust—it is so simple yet looks homemade. Of course if you are the baking type and you like making your own pastry, try the Basic Flaky Double Piecrust on page 209. Either way this pie will come out as pretty as a picture. It tastes as good as it looks too.

3	pounds mixed apples, peeled, cored, and thinly sliced
¾	cup granulated sugar
2	tablespoons cornstarch
	Finely grated zest of 1 lemon
1	tablespoon freshly squeezed lemon juice
¾	teaspoon ground cinnamon
	Pinch salt
	All-purpose flour for dusting
1	15-ounce package rolled refrigerated unbaked piecrusts (2 crusts)
2	tablespoons unsalted butter, cut into small pieces
	Milk for brushing
	Raw sugar for sprinkling

1. Preheat oven to 425°F. Line a rimmed baking sheet with aluminum foil; set aside. In a large bowl, stir together the apples, granulated sugar, cornstarch, lemon zest, lemon juice, cinnamon, and salt; set aside.

2. On a lightly floured surface, roll dough into two 11-inch circles. Line a 9-inch pie plate with one of the piecrusts. Using a sharp knife, cut the remaining piecrust into ¹/₂-inch-wide strips.

3. Spoon the apple mixture into the pie plate and scatter the butter pieces over the apples. Arrange the piecrust strips in a lattice pattern on top. Fold the edges of the bottom crust up to meet the edges of the strips; pinch together to seal and crimp decoratively.

4. Brush the crust lightly with milk and sprinkle with raw sugar. Place pie on the prepared baking sheet. Bake for 20 minutes. Reduce oven temperature to 375°F. Bake about 40 minutes more or until golden and bubbling. Let cool at least 10 minutes before cutting and serving.

MAKES 8 TO 10 SERVINGS

Bittersweet Chocolate Cream Pie

Chocolate pie was always Dad's favorite, so Mama made it pretty regularly, which was fine by us! We make ours with twice the amount of dark chocolate, and it turns out so creamy, rich, and good that it is nearly impossible to stop eating.

¾	cup sugar
¼	cup cornstarch
4	egg yolks
½	teaspoon salt
2	cups milk
1	tablespoon unsalted butter
1	teaspoon vanilla
7	ounces bittersweet chocolate, coarsely chopped
1	prepared single piecrust, baked according to package directions, or Prebaked Piecrust (see recipe, page 209)
	Sweetened whipped cream
	Shaved chocolate

1. In a medium heavy saucepan, whisk together the sugar, cornstarch, egg yolks, and salt. Whisk in the milk. Cook over low heat for 10 to 15 minutes or until thickened to the consistency of pudding, stirring constantly. Strain the custard into a bowl. Stir in the butter and vanilla until butter is melted.

2. In the top of a double boiler set over simmering water, melt the chocolate, stirring until smooth. Fold one-fourth of the chocolate into the custard, then fold in the remaining chocolate. Spoon the filling into the piecrust. Chill for at least 2 hours or until set. Before serving, top with whipped cream and chocolate shavings.

MAKES 8 TO 10 SERVINGS

Sweet Potato Meringue Pie

When we were kids Mom and Dad started a garden. We grew all sorts of things, including sweet potatoes, which we call yams in the South. We grew up with yams and always put butter and cinnamon on top before baking them. This pie is the dessert version of that simple side dish. The meringue sends it over the top.

2	large sweet potatoes, baked and cooled
1	cup sour cream
1	cup granulated sugar
3	large eggs, separated
2	tablespoons unsalted butter, melted
2	tablespoons bourbon
1	teaspoon vanilla
½	teaspoon ground ginger
¼	teaspoon ground nutmeg
¼	teaspoon salt
	All-purpose flour for dusting
1	Basic Flaky Single Piecrust (see recipe, page 208), chilled, or ½ of a 15-ounce package rolled refrigerated unbaked piecrusts (1 crust)
¼	teaspoon cream of tartar
½	cup superfine sugar

1. Preheat oven to 350°F. Peel the potatoes and place in a large mixing bowl. Add the sour cream. Beat on medium speed with an electric mixer until smooth. Beat in the granulated sugar, egg yolks, butter, bourbon, vanilla, ginger, nutmeg, and salt.

2. On a lightly floured surface, roll dough into an 11-inch circle. Line a 9-inch pie plate with the piecrust and crimp the edges decoratively. Pour the sweet potato mixture into the piecrust. Bake for 45 to 55 minutes or until almost set in the center. Let pie cool to room temperature.

3. Place the egg whites and cream of tartar in a second large mixing bowl. Beat on medium-high speed with an electric mixer until soft peaks form (tips curl). Add the superfine sugar, 1 tablespoon at a time, beating until the egg whites are stiff and glossy but not dry. Spoon the meringue over the pie filling; make sure to spread the meringue to the edges and use a spatula to form the customary meringue peaks. Bake at 350°F about 10 minutes or until the meringue is golden. Let pie cool before cutting and serving.

MAKES 8 TO 10 SERVINGS

Hazelnut Dream Bars

We love hazelnut coffee so much that we created a dessert bar to go with it. The taste is a little like those great candies that have a crispy shell, a creamy chocolate filling, and a hazelnut in the center. These bars are perfect for holidays—or any day.

CRUST:

1	cup all-purpose flour
1/3	cup packed brown sugar
	Pinch salt
1/2	cup (1 stick) unsalted butter, cut into pieces

FILLING:

2	large eggs
1	cup packed brown sugar
2	tablespoons all-purpose flour
1	teaspoon vanilla
1/2	teaspoon baking powder
3/4	cup shredded coconut
3/4	cup chopped hazelnuts
3/4	cup miniature semisweet chocolate chips

1. Preheat oven to 350°F. For the crust, in a food processor, pulse together the flour, sugar, and salt. Pulse in the butter until just combined. Press the dough evenly over the bottom of an ungreased 13×9-inch baking pan. Bake about 10 minutes or until golden.

2. For the filling, whisk together the eggs, sugar, flour, vanilla, and baking powder. Stir in the coconut, hazelnuts, and chocolate chips. Spread the filling over the hot crust. Bake about 20 minutes more or until dark golden.

MAKES ABOUT 24 BARS

Espresso Nut Blondies

Chewy, chock-full bars like these are perfect in a lunch box or any time you're on the go. Watch out if you get stuck at home with them because the pan seems to keep calling you back!

1	pound (2¼ cups) dark brown sugar
¾	cup (1½ sticks) unsalted butter, plus additional for coating pan
1	tablespoon instant espresso powder
1	tablespoon hot water
2	large eggs
1½	tablespoons vanilla
2	cups all-purpose flour
2	teaspoons baking powder
½	teaspoon salt
1½	cups semisweet chocolate chips
1	cup toasted walnuts

1. In a medium saucepan, heat the sugar and the ¾ cup butter over medium heat until melted, stirring occasionally. Dissolve the espresso powder in the hot water; stir into the sugar mixture. Let cool.

2. Preheat oven to 350°F. Butter an 11×7-inch baking pan; set aside.

3. Beat the eggs and vanilla into the cooled sugar mixture. In a medium bowl, whisk together the flour, baking powder, and salt; stir into the sugar mixture. Fold in the chocolate chips and walnuts.

4. Spread the mixture evenly in the prepared pan. Bake for 25 to 30 minutes or until golden brown. Transfer to a wire rack to cool completely.

MAKES ABOUT 18 BARS

Double-Fudge Bread Pudding

The only thing better than fudge is double fudge. So what could be better than Double-Fudge Bread Pudding? We add bourbon, which gives desserts a different, distinct flavor, and, of course, plenty of chocolate. This is one of Brooke's favorites.

	Butter for coating dish
1	1-pound loaf day-old French or Italian bread, cut into cubes (about 15 cups)
1	pound semisweet chocolate, grated
1	cup granulated sugar
¾	cup packed light brown sugar
¼	cup unsweetened cocoa powder
1½	teaspoons ground cinnamon
	Pinch salt
6	large eggs
1	tablespoon vanilla
3	cups milk
¼	cup heavy cream
¼	cup bourbon
	Sweetened whipped cream

1. Butter a 13×9-inch baking dish. Spread the bread cubes in the prepared dish. Place the grated chocolate in a medium bowl; set aside.

2. In a large bowl, whisk together the sugars, cocoa powder, cinnamon, and salt. Whisk in the eggs, one at a time. Stir in the vanilla.

3. In a medium saucepan, bring the milk and cream to a boil. Pour the mixture over the grated chocolate and stir until the chocolate is completely melted. Whisking constantly, slowly pour the chocolate mixture into the egg mixture. Stir in the bourbon. Pour the chocolate mixture evenly over the bread cubes. Refrigerate pudding for at least 1 hour or up to 12 hours, stirring occasionally.

4. Preheat oven to 325°F. Bake the pudding about 1 hour or until just set and a knife inserted in the center of the pudding comes out clean. Serve the pudding warm or chilled with whipped cream.

MAKES 12 SERVINGS

Pink Lemonade Layer Cake

Jamie: Brooke and I saw this cake at a bakery in Savannah, and I thought it was so fabulous that Bobby and I worked with the recipe until we had it just the way we wanted: tart and sweet at the same time. This is a great summertime dessert.

CAKE:

Butter for coating pans
1   18.25-ounce white cake mix
3   tablespoons pink lemonade
     drink powder
3   eggs
⅓   cup vegetable oil
1   teaspoon finely grated lemon zest

FROSTING:

1   pound confectioners' (powdered) sugar
½   cup (1 stick) unsalted butter, softened
3   tablespoons frozen pink lemonade
     concentrate
1   teaspoon vanilla
1   teaspoon finely grated lemon zest

1. Preheat oven to 350°F. Butter two 8-inch round cake pans and line the bottoms with parchment paper or waxed paper; set aside.

2. For the cake, in a large bowl, stir together the cake mix and lemonade powder. Prepare the cake batter according to the package directions, using the eggs and oil. Stir the lemon zest into the batter. Pour the batter evenly into the prepared pans. Bake for 30 to 35 minutes or until golden and a toothpick inserted in the centers of the cakes comes out clean. Let the cakes cool in the pans for 10 minutes. Carefully turn cakes out onto a wire rack to cool completely.

3. For the frosting, beat together the confectioners' sugar and butter until fluffy. Beat in the remaining frosting ingredients until combined.

4. Transfer one cake to a cake stand or large platter. Using an offset spatula, spread the top of the cake with a layer of frosting. Place the second cake on top of the first. Spread the remaining frosting over the top and sides of both layers.

MAKES 10 TO 12 SERVINGS

Chocolate Chunk Cookies

Mama always put M&Ms in her chocolate chip cookies, and we could see the candy colors all through them when they were baked. We would try to break them apart so that there was candy in every bite. Even when we make these cookies today, that kidlike excitement comes right back.

1½	cups walnuts, chopped
2¼	cups all-purpose flour
1	teaspoon baking soda
1	teaspoon salt
1	cup (2 sticks) unsalted butter, softened
¾	cup granulated sugar
¾	cup packed light brown sugar
2	teaspoons vanilla
2	large eggs
8	ounces bittersweet chocolate (at least 60 percent cacao), coarsely chopped
1	cup candy-coated milk chocolate candies

1. Position oven racks in the top and bottom thirds of the oven. Preheat oven to 325°F. Spread the walnuts on a rimmed baking sheet; toast on the top rack of the oven for 7 to 10 minutes or until fragrant and golden, shaking the pan once to ensure even toasting. Transfer to a small bowl; set aside.

2. Increase the oven temperature to 375°F. In a medium bowl, stir together the flour, baking soda, and salt.

3. In a large mixing bowl, beat butter and sugars on medium speed with an electric mixer for 2 to 3 minutes or until pale and fluffy. Beat in vanilla. Beat in the eggs, one at a time, beating well after each addition and scraping down sides of the bowl as necessary. Beat in the flour mixture until incorporated. Stir in the walnuts, chocolate, and candies.

4. Drop dough by heaping teaspoonfuls 2 inches apart onto two ungreased cookie sheets. Bake on separate racks in the oven for 9 to 11 minutes or until golden brown, switching pan positions halfway through baking. Let cookies cool on sheets for 2 minutes. Transfer to wire racks to cool completely.

MAKES ABOUT 7 DOZEN COOKIES

Basic Flaky Single Piecrust

1¼   cups all-purpose flour
¼   teaspoon salt
7   tablespoons unsalted butter, chilled and cut into small pieces
2   tablespoons shortening
2   to 3 tablespoons ice water

1. In a food processor or large bowl, pulse or whisk together the flour and salt. Pulse or cut in the butter and shortening until the mixture resembles coarse crumbs. Pulse or cut in enough ice water until dough just comes together (it should not be sticky).

2. Press the dough into a ball; using the palm of your hand, flatten it into a disk. Wrap disk tightly in plastic wrap. Chill for 1 hour or until ready to use.

MAKES ONE 9-INCH PIECRUST

"There's always room for pie!"
—Bobby

Basic Flaky Double Piecrust

2½ cups all-purpose flour
½   teaspoon salt
14 tablespoons unsalted butter, chilled and cut into small pieces
¼   cup shortening
3   to 5 tablespoons ice water

1. In a food processor or large bowl, pulse or whisk together the flour and salt. Pulse or cut in the butter and shortening until the mixture resembles coarse crumbs. Pulse or cut in enough ice water until dough just comes together (it should not be sticky).

2. Press the dough into a large ball. Divide the dough into two smaller balls; using the palm of your hand, flatten each ball into a disk. Wrap disks tightly in plastic wrap. Chill for 1 hour or until ready to use.

MAKES TWO 9-INCH PIECRUSTS

Prebaked Piecrust

    All-purpose flour for dusting
1   Basic Flaky Single Piecrust (see recipe, page 208)
    Pie weights or dried beans

1. Preheat oven to 375°F. On a lightly floured surface, roll dough into an 11-inch circle. Line a 9-inch pie plate with dough. Prick the bottom of the piecrust all over with a fork. Trim off any excess dough and crimp the edges decoratively.

2. Line the bottom and sides of the piecrust with aluminum foil. Pour pie weights or several cups of dried beans into the foil, evenly distributing the weights.

3. Bake for 20 minutes. Remove the weights and foil. Bake for 5 to 10 minutes more or until pale golden.

MAKES ONE 9-INCH PIECRUST

Buckeyes

Buckeyes are basically peanut butter dunked in melted chocolate. When we were kids, Mama always made a big batch around Christmastime for our teachers. We joke that Jamie made it through middle school only because of Mama's desserts.

3   cups confectioners' (powdered) sugar
1   cup creamy peanut butter
¼   cup (½ stick) unsalted butter, softened
1   teaspoon vanilla
3   cups semisweet chocolate chips
50   toothpicks

1. Line a large baking sheet with parchment paper; set aside.

2. In the bowl of an electric mixer fitted with a paddle attachment, beat together the sugar, peanut butter, butter, and vanilla. (The dough should be slightly crumbly.) Roll the dough into 1-inch balls. Transfer the balls to the prepared baking sheet and stick a toothpick into each ball. Place the sheet in the freezer and chill for 30 minutes to an hour.

3. In the top of a double boiler set over simmering water, melt the chocolate chips, stirring until smooth. Hold a ball by the toothpick and place a fork under the ball to stabilize it while you dip. Dip the ball in the chocolate, leaving a small hole of peanut butter showing at the top of the ball as the "buckeye." Let the excess chocolate drip back into the pot. Return the buckeye to the baking sheet. Repeat with remaining balls.

4. Cover loosely with plastic wrap and refrigerate for at least 2 hours or overnight.

MAKES ABOUT 48 PIECES

U

V

W

Z

Celebrations

Enjoy!